Let me explain the title. During our t
had posters printed, reading "Paris
fantastically original I accept but ste
or bust theme which people of my gᴜ.ᴜᵣᴜ.ᴜᴜ. ᴡᴜ.
recognise. There I was, in my yellow lycra and huge top
hat when a chap said to me, "where's Bust"? I obviously
looked as puzzled as I felt, because he nodded to the
poster. Ah Ha! A wit. Rapier fast, I shot back, "just above
the waist", boom boom! Now *he* looked puzzled and,
when I looked into his eyes I saw ....nothing. Far
from exchanging banter with a fellow fun loving witster, I
was talking to a man who thought that both Bust and
Waist were places. In France obviously, like Paris, he
wasn't that daft but he couldn't quite place them
somehow. Anyway, his enquiry was actually whether we
were heading for Paris, or Bust. Chucking Waist into the
equation sent him into meltdown I fear.

Foreword.

This attempt at a book was inspired by several things. Firstly my wife and partner in cycling, Jayne, went on for four years about it. Anyone who knows Jayne will realise what a determined effort it was to resist for four years. In my defence, for two of those years I was still working and for the following eighteen months I was renovating a shell we had purchased in France and retired to. Obviously I don't literally mean a shell, that would be stupid, but a house with four walls and a roof but precious little else. Hard work but satisfying, especially considering that it was all we could afford. We aren't City types who quit high flying megabucks jobs to "find ourselves", Mr and Mrs Ordinary are in the building. There is still much to do but it's minus four outside, there's a roaring log fire going and it seems like a good time to start.

I've had a very interesting and varied career, starting off in Sales and ending up in Nursing, with loads of ups and downs in between. Some of the ups were pretty high and some of the lows, pretty low. The final years as a Marie Curie Nurse made a huge impression on me. They certainly made me realise that, despite what I've just said, my lows were nothing compared to some. I think I knew this within me but there's nothing like having it slapped around your face to drive it home. I saw the best and worst of people. Families with so much love that it broke my heart and families so dysfunctional that it broke my heart.

In between chapters I'm going to relate some stories, share some families' experiences and hopefully give an insight into why I felt ·so driven to raise money for Marie Curie Cancer Care, as it was then called. There will also be some mentions within the body of the text where relevant. Clearly, the faces and voices of the contributors will be disguised for their protection.

I'm not sure what to call these little asides but for now I'm using "reflections". If you can think of anything better do please let me know.

Prologue:

As we stopped at the traffic lights in the shadow of the Eiffel Tower, a female voice behind me said, "we've only gone and bloody well done it"! It just *may* have been Holly. I'm not certain but the fact that I heard it so clearly above all the Parisian traffic makes me think it perhaps was. I'm not saying her voice is loud……..
Anyway, whoever it was that said it, was right, we had gone and bloody well done it! Two old (in my opinion), overweight (in everyone's opinion), couch potatoes, had cycled from London to Paris. Two hundred miles, as near as makes no difference, over three of the hottest days of 2014.

So how the heck did that happen I hear you ask? Well don't be so bloody impatient, you can see that I'm doing it and I'm going as fast as I can so just wait until it's finished then buy the book!

It began either in November 2012 or July 2013, depending on how you look at it. November 2012 was when Jayne, one of the two old overweight folk, said she'd like a bike so she could do some exercise. She had been a keen swimmer but shoulder problems (obviously age related), put paid to that. Being a dutiful Husband Steve, the second even older of the overweight folk, got her one for Christmas. Along with all sorts of other richly deserved luxurious gifts, obviously. The bike got it's first outing in Spring and Jayne was hooked. The first ride was 2 miles of the flattest country Lincolnshire, which is pretty much all flat,has to offer. It took her about half an hour and she came back looking like Paula Radcliffe in the Athens Marathon. I was sympathetic of course and extra sympathetic the next day, when she found that her legs belonged to someone else and wouldn't do as she asked. The result of my sympathy was a gauntlet, firmly slapped in my face and thrown to the ground at my feet. Being a Man, I of course picked up the gauntlet and thirty minutes later, regretted it. I *told* Jayne that I'd done the same trip as her. I lied. It was a good thing we only had the one bike at the time or she would have followed and seen me turn round at the halfway point! I fell off the bike very gracefully on my return and explained to Jayne that Men always dismounted that way. My own legs stopped obeying me instantly; no waiting 24 hours like Jayne's. And here's an interesting thing; Jayne had no sympathy whatsoever! There was a distinct air of, "I told you so" about her, which was most unbecoming I thought. Jayne continued cycling periodically; I retired.

July is Le Tour de France month! One of our favourite events. We love everything French and watch it every year as a travel programme, watching out for places we know and for ideas of new places to visit. 2013 however was different. Jayne was now a cyclist! We watched with new eyes and when Chris Froome burst into the lead and held it for the second British win in succession, Jayne was elated. As we watched them ride down the Champs Elysee, Jayne uttered the fateful words. The words that changed our lives and ruled our lives for the next year. "Wouldn't it be amazing to do that"? Someone then said something stupid. "You can do it, they organise Charity events. Marie Curie do it". We hit the internet immediately and within half an hour we'd paid our entry fees and were committed! Oh hell, what had we done? I was no longer retired; I was a cyclist.

My first Marie Curie reflection follows on the next page and explains far better than I ever could, why it is such a wonderful cause.

Dear Steve,

We would like to say a heartfelt thank you for the sensitivity and care you showed to our mum, Mary ~~████~~ during the last weeks of her life and expressing for the help and support you provided. You went above and beyond, arriving early and leaving late and we appreciate immensely the continued reassurance and help in keeping his calm during that time.

You know without us saying how mum very much valued your care and attention. That is to have your friendly face to help us over the last few nights with mum, helped us cope so much better than we would have had you personally not been there.

Keep up the good work Steve, you are a real gem and we wish that everyone had a 'Steve' to look after them in their final days.

Good luck to you in the future.

With love from

Anne.

Carole,

Vayne.

xxx

Chapter one.

In the beginning:

I'm a Marie Curie Cancer Care nurse, working with terminally ill patients who have elected to die in their own homes. It's a privilege that I value above anything to be able to make the last days and hours of a life just a little easier, for the patient themselves and also their families and loved ones. Of course it's often very sad but the positive response of everyone concerned makes it so worthwhile. When the thought of the ride first cropped up there was obviously no doubt about who would be benefiting from the money raised. Our commitment was for £2,900. This worried Jayne but I always had faith that we would achieve it comfortably. Looking back, we had no idea just how much this event would take over our lives. In the early days I spent hours on end trawling the internet and sending off cheeky emails to organisations and Companies, begging them to donate items to be auctioned or used as raffle prizes. A complete list of corporate donors is included later and I would like to take this opportunity to thank every single one of them again. We'll touch on the fundraising in more detail but there are some who deserve extra, extra special thanks. The Management and staff of Adults Supporting Adults, the not for profit Charity for which Jayne worked, were amazing! They accounted for probably 50% of the total raised and supported every one of our events to the full. Our good friends Harry and Shelley, of the Oriental Palace Restaurant in Boston, turned the place over to us one Saturday and laid on a superb feast for around 50 of us. They and the ever cheerful Sam, made the event great fun and very profitable; for us but certainly not for them. Right at the top of the list though, is Steppin' Stones. We came across them at a local event where they were playing and we loved their music. We took a card, thinking we could perhaps persuade them to play for us at a reduced rate, considering the cause we were supporting. I sent off the trademark cheeky email suggesting the same and was amazed to get a message straight back telling me that their fee would be cups of tea and coffee! They played for several hours at the Oriental Palace and in passing, mentioned that they also did Barn Dances, with a caller and all the trimmings. We were sold immediately and try as we might, we could not persuade them to accept a fee for that either. The dance was a huge success, enjoyed by all and because of their generosity in refusing a fee, we added nicely to the kitty. It was without doubt the event of the year and is still talked about to this day. We discovered that evening that our daughter Ellie is not only a barn dance/ ceilidh diva but also a bit of a stern taskmaster. Somehow, her brain just seems to get it. While others are tying themselves up in knots and falling over each other, Ellie grasps it straight away and, being the expert she obviously was, she assumed the role of team leader and teacher. Teacher may be stretching a bit; Obergruppenfuhrer is perhaps better. Her "tips" began as just that but before long they became exasperated cries of, "are you a man? It's the man that does that not the woman"!   "Why don't you just listen?! It's not hard"!   It was hilarious and we loved it. I "danced" all night in my lycra and thanked heaven that I was in training or I would have expired!   What fantastic people and talented musicians with a great repertoire. Anyone with an event to organise in or around Lincolnshire look no further; Steppin' Stones.

The general consensus when we told people what we were doing was that we had finally taken leave of our senses. Many were convinced that we would never do it. "WHAT! 200 miles for old fat folk? Can't be done"! That reaction was understandable but actually just what we needed. We are both a bit contrary and the one way to make sure that we do something is to say that we can't!

I dragged Jayne's Son's old bike out of the garage and fixed it up and we were in training. The last time I'd ridden a bike was 45 years ago and it was a fixed wheel. This, although we later found out was not a great bike, had 21 gears. This caused some early problems. Initially I was very wobbly. Whoever said that you never forget how to ride a bike was wrong. You *do* forget, not completely but enough to make it extremely dangerous! It took some time to master the gears. I kept getting mixed up as to which way to flick the switch and even which switch to flick. The result was that I was trying to change from first to eighteenth in one go, or even more dangerous, the other way around. I switched accidentally into lowest gear available and my legs were whizzing round like Michael Flatley on speed. I then decided that I needed to look at the gear switches as I changed, so avoiding that sort of problem. A sound plan I thought. However, it turned out that as I looked down to change gear, I stopped steering in a straight line. Luckily, the hedge is a big one, quite soft and will recover quickly. After a day or two I was getting the hang of it and I felt ready to hit the road; literally!

Jayne of course, had a start. Initially we went on different rides because she was so much fitter. I started with the original two miles and it felt like 200. When I got to the T Junction at the end of the road on the way back, I wasn't sure I had the strength to pedal over the road to make the right turn safely, so I finished the ride on the pavement! Naughty of me I know and looking back, rather sad at the physical state I'd let myself get into. This continued for about ten days, then I extended the ride to three miles and soon after that to a six mile loop which included what passes for a hill here in Lincolnshire. We were cycling together by then; Jayne waiting patiently for me every couple of miles. Yes, she was that much faster than me and much fitter. I've always joked about her powerful thighs, saying that she could get a job with the R.A.F. kickstarting aircraft, but they have come in handy! The first time I encountered that hill I was convinced that my life expectancy was now measured in seconds rather than years. I was in what we later found out was called by proper cyclists, the Granny Gear, the lowest you can get. For every revolution of the pedals, forward motion was a couple of inches. Pedestrians were speeding past me and progress was so slow that I was wobbling around like a drunk on a unicycle. But I reached the summit and lived to tell the tale. From that day on, hills and I were mortal enemies. My brain made me panic and my legs just turned into lactic acid containers. God, how I hated hills. I still do, even though I'm much better at them now. I can get 80% of the way up in Jayne's shadow but that last 20% does for me every time. I'm ashamed to say that my hill climbing technique is based upon swearing. I start fairly safely with the odd, "damn thing", building up through "bloody", maybe a "shit" or two, before losing it completely with words I won't go into today but if any of you have cycled with me you will be familiar with them all. Sometimes, as I reach the summit, I've been known to let out a primeval roar of "TAKE THAT YOU ******* ******** ********** HILL"! Jayne is way ahead by this time, steaming down the other side and virtually, sometimes in fact literally, out of sight. Occasionally she asked whether I heard the roar whilst she was going down the hill, wondering what it might be. Eventually she realised it was me and made sure she was even further ahead; to avoid embarrassment.

That first attempt at the loop, as we called it, was on August 20th 2013. It's 6.8 miles and took me 45 minutes at an average speed of 8.9 mph. On March 4th 2014, it took 28 minutes at an average speed of just over 14 mph! I still hated that and every other hill but I was out of Granny gear and not dreading it quite so much. To put the issue in context, I must add that Jayne on her own would have done the loop about 4-5 minutes quicker than when waiting for me and the majority of the people who took part in the ride, "the Peloton", would have done it probably 10 minutes faster. I'm not saying I was the weakest link but during the ride they all kept winking at me for some reason. Very odd behaviour. In my day a wink meant something very different; I hope. One surprising problem we encountered was neck ache. In hindsight I guess that it's not so surprising, with the head held in an unnatural position for the first time in years. Initially we had to stop every four or five miles to massage each others necks. Passing motorists must have been rather puzzled by two ancient cyclists engaged in foreplay.

Early on, I had severe buttock problems. I let my mean streak take hold when buying cycling shorts. Cheap, in the world of padded shorts, is not good! The saddle had a gel cover, which didn't do the job. I added a second gel on top of the first and that didn't help. On our first really long ride, as we thought of it then, I was in agony after 12 miles. I felt ready to weep and could hardly walk. In an inspired moment, Jayne persuaded me to ditch the gel covers. My first reaction was that she must hate me and wanted me to suffer more but she put forward a reasoned argument which went something like, "I'm fed up with your moaning. If it hurts so much the bloody things are doing no good anyway so just get rid of them and give me some peace". Like most men, I know when to do as I'm told and when I can get away with a show of defiance. This was definitely a do as you're told moment. It worked! Apparently the gels were making the seat too fat and stopping me settle into it properly. On the ride back home I was much better and once I'd recovered (and ditched my mean streak and bought better shorts),I never had buttock trouble again. She's a clever old thing.

This event also led to a fun night at work. I was with a Patient I had looked after before and had got to know her family quite well. Usually, there was a very comfy chair for me just outside their Mum's room but on this night they had been overrun by visitors and the chair had been taken downstairs, to be replaced with a dining chair. The Daughters apologised profusely and of course I made nothing of it. After an hour, or maybe even less, my backside was killing me. It was agony and I still had 8 hours to go. I knew I couldn't manage that, so I got onto the floor and lay on my side reading my book. The look on the Daughters face as she came out of her room to pop to the loo was a picture. My mind raced through all kinds of good reasons as to why I should be in this position on their landing but actually, none of them seemed any good at all. I told the truth as tactfully as possible, to much amusement. The story found it's way around the family and my bottom was the source of many enquiries after that. The postscript is that when the lovely lady sadly passed away, I received a very generous donation from the three daughters. The message attached read, " In memory of our Mum and the priceless care given in our time of need. The vision of you laying down because you couldn't sit after too much cycling practice, will stay in our minds forever Steve". All my Patients are special to me but I am a Human Being as well as a nurse, with the weaknesses which that brings. The memory of that Patient and her family will also stay with me forever.

Having learnt from my cheapskate mistakes, I bought an expensive pair of long cycling tights for the cooler times. You ladies will understand my dilemma later. We were on a ride through a village quite near home when Jayne decided to stop. Just stop. No reason, no indication of her intention whatsoever. Just stop. I also managed to stop, just in time and was about to make my feelings known in a very clear manner, when I fell off! Gusset trouble. I've never had gusset trouble because I don't normally wear tights. In a very masculine and athletic way, I threw my right leg over the saddle. In the throwing over process however, the gusset problem manifested itself, and the droopy bit in the middle caught up in the nose of my saddle and I ended up on the deck with "Boris" on top of me. Jayne's howl of laughter could be heard in the Arctic circle. She's a rat bag, but you already knew that.

We trained quite scientifically most of the time, gradually building up distance and searching out as many hills (yes, hills), as we could find. Quite early on in the programme we were introduced to Jack. Jack runs Pedal-tech of Heckington and is a bike mechanic of the highest order and a man generous to a fault. When he learnt the cause we were cycling for he refused to accept any payment for his time, charging us only for parts. One of Jack's early pieces of advice was, "get rid of those bikes, you need something a bit better if you're going to get to Paris". Having already spent £400 on registering for the event and around £100 on kit, (soon to rise to several times that amount as we got rid of the first rubbish we bought), we were a little budget light. Skint in other words. That's what credit cards are for, so off we went to our local cycle shop and bought two new bikes; £500. In hindsight, which is something Jayne has in 20/20, we should really have spent a bit more. I'm not saying you need a top notch bike to do this type of challenge but an extra £50 or so would have made quite a difference in areas like weight and rolling resistance. There were bikes on the event valued from £1,000 to over £7,000! My machine became "Boris", it was during all the publicity for the Boris Bikes in London and although I'm not saying I support his Politics, he is good for a laugh.** Jayne's became, "Oh shit". That's what she called out when she fell very slowly and delicately into a patch of nettles on our first ride out on them. Once she'd recovered from the trademark Jayne howl of laughter, we dragged her out of the stingers and went looking for Dock leaves. To be fair to Jayne, it's only me that calls her bike "Oh shit". She is far too much the lady! After a few sessions on the new steeds we decided to tackle the one real hill anywhere near us, the A52 heading out of Grantham. There are people who will scoff but to me it was tackling Everest. The one saving grace is that it has a McDonald's at the bottom. I'm not a huge fan of any of the fast food chains actually, with the exception of McDonald's breakfast. The sausage and egg McMuffin is a thing of beauty. Perfectly seasoned and delicious. We timed our arrival to make sure to catch breakfast service, for a reason I don't understand or agree with they stop the sausage McPerfect at either ten or half past; at least twelve hours too early. We dismounted, being Grantham we locked up the bikes, and praying that the sight of us in Lycra didn't put the clientele off their breakfast, we headed for the door.

It was at this point that I was attacked by a car. I had done nothing to provoke it, other than wear Lycra and I accept that there is a school of thought which regards this as sufficient provocation for far worse. My first thought was that some silly woman was reversing at me, a thing which women do willy nilly in my experience. On closer examination I saw that the car was, in fact, in sole charge of itself and certainly proceeding without due care and attention! Heading for a busy main road as it was, I thought it best to intervene. I chucked my considerable weight behind it and managed to stop it rolling, while Jayne rushed inside to locate the owner. The previously predicted silly woman appeared, unlocked the door and yanked the handbrake on. Very flustered she started screaming, "my babies, my babies"! Newspaper headlines flashed before my eyes. "Hero cyclist saves twins from certain death"! "Marie Curie angel in heroic rescue"! "Anyone would have done the same says modest hero"! Bloody hell, I'm going to be front page news in my bloody Lycra. Silly woman runs round to the back door and reveals a cage containing puppies. People who know me will testify that I'm very partial to dogs and who doesn't love a puppy? At this point it is important to qualify my silly woman comments. Those views are not genuinely held but included simply to add a bit of controversy. Having now explained I expect the controversy to be finished with, making it's inclusion pointless. Oh well.

Rescue duties duly performed, it's time for breakfast.

One *double* sausage and egg McMuffin with extra hash brown later and we're off. This hill is two miles long, through which we climb two hundred feet according to google maps. At this point part of me wants to get that worked out as a gradient, whilst the other is saying, "don't be stupid, you've not done maths for 50 years and haven't a clue where to start"! The problem is that it's not a constant gradient, really quite shallow at the start and again at the end, with the wicked bit in the middle. I never listen to the sensible side so here we go. I remember clearly in maths lessons, that the word "assume" was used. So I'm going to assume that the beginning and end bits equal one of the two miles but only fifty of the feet climbed. One hundred and fifty feet in one mile is where the calculations start. See, It's going well already! Now, a mile contains 1,760 yards if I remember correctly and each yard has three feet, therefore a mile is five thousand two hundred and eighty feet. It's getting tricky now, where do I go from here? Do I divide 5,280 by 150? If so, that's 35.2. Does that mean it's 1:35? If so that's nonsense, it's much worse than that!

Whatever the gradient is, it's very tough but we made it. All the way to the top, cycling every inch! Woo hoo! Yet again my vocabulary was used freely and at full volume but it got me to the top.

*

Since writing that I have revised my opinion. Sorry if I offend anyone with a different view of Boris but events have shown he's not just a bumbling idiot but also a fibber.

Marie Curie reflection.

I'm getting the negative out of the way because I don't want it to spoil anything later on, but it would be wrong to pretend that everything is always good.

I arrived at the Patient's home and was let in by a family member and introduced to the four other people in the room, which turned out to be two Sons, two Daughters in Law and one Daughter of the Patient. I went through to Mrs. S, the Patient and introduced myself and performed the required checks and observations.

I began to get slightly concerned when the family came in and asked if I wanted a drink. Usually this is tea or coffee, so I accepted but the concern began when I was offered a beer or a short! After explaining that it would be inappropriate there was no further offer of a soft drink or hot beverage.

An hour or so later the noise began. It started as a buzz in the background but soon developed into raised voices. I did my best to ignore it but eventually the noise became so loud that I went into the room and asked them to quieten down, for the sake of their Mother. Suitably chastened, they duly shut up.

For about half an hour. Shouting drifted through the house and I heard, "you're not having that, she's always promised that to me"! "Oh no she didn't, everyone knows she said I was having it"! Followed by a crash, followed by, "you ****, you've broken it you stupid cow"! Followed by screeching and screaming like I've never heard. Now I was angry! I stormed through to find three piles of household goods and ornaments, clearly sorted into "Mine when she's dead", piles. A shattered porcelain dog so horribly tacky was all over the floor, clearly the cause of the preceding argument. The two Sisters in Law and the Sister were wrestling over the remains of the dog while the two brothers sat ignoring everything whilst supping beer, surrounded by empty bottles.

I lost it. I'm sorry and a little ashamed to admit it, but I lost it. I berated them soundly for their behaviour in front of a total stranger and their dying Mother. The two men had the grace to look sheepish but the women flew into a rage, all squabbling forgiven, uniting against a common foe; me! Having had the pleasure of playing a good deal of rugby, my knowledge of bad language is extensive. I don't think I heard anything for the first time that night but it was a first in that context. The two brothers eventually succeeded in shutting the women up and went so far as to eject their two wives from the house. Brave isn't the word but maybe it was par for the course. The two evictees refused to go quietly and continued screaming abuse through the letterbox and banging on doors and windows. I explained to them that if this continued I would remove myself from the premises, leaving the care of my patient to them. The response was as follows, "you step out this ******* door and we'll ******* stab ya, ya ******* pervert"! One can only assume that all male nurses are perverts in their eyes, or perhaps it was the fact that these women were so highly desirable that they got fed up with the unwanted attention and got their retaliation in first. Probably that one actually, their beauty was only matched by their charm and grace.

I called the Police, who duly arrived and told me that it was a well known family in the area and they advised me that it would not be safe to remain alone in the house. They took no action against anyone that night but they escorted me to my car and saw me off safely. That behaviour resulted in Marie Curie withdrawing nursing care on safety grounds and I can only hope that nasty things happened to all of them, particularly the sisters in law. Not too nasty of course.

CHAPTER 2

Give us the Money!

Once we'd signed up, the process got going pretty quickly. We were contacted by the fundraising team and once they found out that I was a Marie Curie nurse, they shifted into overdrive. Our local Fundraising Manager, Dawn Broomfield, arranged local Press coverage and came over to supervise us posing in silly hats for the Papers. She also organised facebook coverage on the Marie Curie Cancer Care, East Midlands page.

The Head Office team also sent through at least half a ton of paperwork, all posted separately, all duplicated and including some for other riders. Money saving suggestion sent by return! We were also allocated our two travel guides for the trip, Dan Nelson and Char. I never did get to find out if Char was short for something, whether there was a "lotte" or "maine" missing or perhaps "grilled" or "coal"? We got to know Dan very well over the Months but Char had to pull out of the trip after injuring herself in a bizarre accident. She hit a mattress in her car! Now I don't know what you think but my first thought was that if you've got to hit something, then a mattress is not a bad choice. Better than another car for example, or a bridge. Apparently though, this particular mattress was speeding in a built up area. The mattress was jailed for two years but apparently it escaped, well it was sprung actually . Char was replaced by the accident free Peter Lee. For any Northern town aficionados I think I called him everything but Peterlee! He became used to me shouting out, "Hey Durham", or "watch out Spennymoor"! Dan and Pete were both fantastic lads and as far as I know, still are. They gave great support before and during the event and made sure that we gelled into a very close knit team.

They started the London to Paris facebook page which enabled us to start to build the camaraderie before we'd even met. There were a few regular contributors in the early days and I made it my mission to try to get more people involved so we had issues in common and things to chat about when we eventually met in person. It worked very well as a bonding medium, with many "in" jokes amongst the participants. One of my favourites was a post I made up, telling the crew that a new law had come into force in France, which meant all wheeled vehicles had to carry a fire extinguisher, I urged participants to hurry because I had received information that Halford's were running very low on stock. Other bike shops are available. I didn't catch all of them but a gratifying number messaged me in panic asking for further advice. My main themes were moaning about hills, complaining about how old I was and generally trying to wind people up. As the ride got closer the group expanded and my coconspiritors began to get the hang of the idea. This was the first inkling of the cycling pedigree of the group. Posts contained odd quotes like, " when I did the London to Peking ride last year", or "my favourite ride was through Vietnam and that was when the Yanks were still bombing the crap out of the place; what fun"!! Then a mysterious word "Strava", began to appear. My first thought was that it was an illicit substance used by the Pro's. Several people asked, "was I on Strava"? "Certainly not, I'm clean"! It appears that it's an "app" which records details of rides completed in categories like distance, top speed, average speed, altitude gained, calories burned, maximum gradient climbed etc etc etc. The beauty of this, other than knowing the information oneself, is that it can be shared with other people in order to gain "kudos". Further worries about the company we were about to find ourselves in followed. Here is an app which records my failings and then, to complete my humiliation, shares it with others? **** that! I remember one of my posts was something like, " I've cut down the fags to 30 a day. I never drink more than 5 pints a night and still I'm struggling on hills. Jayne says I should cut out some of my Mistresses but I think that's churlish." Please note that ALL those were jokes! Only 5 pints a night is ridiculous. My suggestion for an app would be one that showed useful information; Pubs on or near the route for example. A hill avoiding route-finder. The best bacon sandwich shop. Please feel free to add your own suggestions in the space provided

....

....

....

....

....

....

....

We'd decided that we wanted the fundraising out of the way as soon as possible because we knew we would have to spend solid hours on the bikes. We were determined to be as fit as possible, so that we would hopefully enjoy the challenge; not collapse in a heap at every stop.

The first event was the aforementioned Oriental Palace Banquet. We know Harry and Shelley very well, having been introduced by my Sister Lesley and her partner Paul. We helped when they opened the Restaurant and have always been regular customers. They organised an unbelievable hot buffet, with everyone's favourite dishes as well as some new things. They were so generous that they can't possibly have covered their costs. One memorable moment stands out from that day. Jayne and I were at the door dressed, as usual, in our yellow lycra. A family, unaware that the restaurant had been given over to the special event, came through the door. Totally unphased, the Dad just asked for a table for four. Here is my question. What on Earth would it have taken to surprise these people, if being greeted at a Chinese Restaurant by two overweight lumps, dressed in dayglo didn't do the job? We explained the situation and, having ample food available, said they were welcome to join us. Join us they did and settled in nicely, actually winning a very nice raffle prize to boot.

As well as ticket sales we ran our main raffle at this event. Again in hindsight, we should have held some prizes back for future events and even auctioned some, rather than included them in the raffle. My cheeky emails had garnered an excellent range of prizes from very generous people and organisations. I will now attempt to name them all!

Fogarty's Quilts. P&O Ferries. DFDS Ferries. Lincolnshire Aviation Heritage Centre. Blackfriars Theatre, Boston. Broadbent Theatre, Louth. West End Cinema, Boston. Oriental Palace Restaurant, Boston. Natureland, Skegness. Lincolnshire Gliding Club,Strubby. Fly 365, Wickenby. Bateman's Brewery, Wainfleet. Tesco, Sleaford. Roz Laggan at Healing Feeling, Louth.

That Lunch raised £400, with the promise of a matching donation from the wonderful Adults Supporting Adults.

Also at this event, I was presented with one of my favourite accessories by our lovely friend Karen. She bought me a very very loud hooter. Forget the bell, this hooter was far more to my personality.

The first money through the door though, was a donation from the lovely Leah Page, a wonderful nurse from Lincoln County Hospital. This came after setting up the "justgiving" page. Justgiving makes it so easy for donors as well as us beggars, with the added bonus that the Chancellor lobs an extra 25% our way from his own pocket. George Osborne is a proper gent! Bless him, it's a good job he's a toff and can afford it. PS Other Chancellors are available.

The next big lump of cash came from our local Primary School. I contacted the Head Teacher, thinking that perhaps we could interest the Pupils in the event and link it with Maths, Geography and Science. Those subjects no longer exist apparently, having been allocated new trendy names so as not to frighten the kids. Be that as it may, Osbournby Primary School became fully involved in the event. Bridgette, the Head Teacher, invited me in to speak to the assembled school during assembly. The children were initially a little frightened by this old fat bloke in yellow lycra. Understandably so, but they soon recovered. They asked a whole range of very interesting questions, ranging from my training routine to what I would do if I needed the toilet. Ah, toilet. Primary school kids just love the word don't they? They then got involved in events for the whole of the second week in January 2014. Lessons were tailored around it, they rode miles and miles on exercise bikes, they had a French Breakfast, with croissants and hot chocolate, a cake sale and many other fundraising initiatives. This school, with just one hundred pupils, raised nearly £500. I'm so grateful to Bridgette, her Staff, Pupils and Parents for that fantastic effort.

As you will already know from the explanation of the title, we'd heard through the L2P facebook page about riders setting up exercise bikes in the foyer of well trodden establishments and strutting their stuff with collecting buckets. Any port in a storm so we decided to try it, figuring that we'd be fundraising and training at the same time. Jayne rightly pointed out the initial flaw in the plan. We didn't have an exercise bike. Now be honest. Whoever you are, reading this, you have at some time had an exercise bike. They are used mainly for hanging clothes on, either because you're not sure you will ever use them again or to wait for the wife to Iron them and put them away for you. The pile increases in size until you actually forget what it is that's holding it up. That's the time to go and get a new exercise bike. Ebay. That's the place to look. We found one advertised not far away and at a price which meant we didn't have to fundraise for it.

What fabulous people! I'm ashamed to say that we've lost their details because they deserve a huge thank you. When they discovered why we needed it, they not only gave it free of charge but made a donation too. Here's some advice. Don't advertise on ebay because you make a loss! Maybe some people don't, but 100% do in my personal experience. I'd love to thank that lovely couple so I'd urge everyone to send an email to everyone in their contacts list asking if they donated their exercise bike to a couple doing a charity ride. The recipients should then do the same and continue through 6 cycles. It's an internet fact that the 6 cycle rule can find anyone in the world. Except maybe in the Amazonian Rainforest. In fact I sincerely hope not in that case.

Exercise bike obtained, we set out blagging our way into various establishments. One of my Patients at this time was a senior area manager for Morrisons Supermarket. During one of our early hours chats the subject came up and his response will never leave me. "I know I've only got a couple of days to live. Contact, name obviously withheld, and tell him I'll haunt him if he doesn't arrange spots in the local Morrisons stores". He was correct in his estimate, as we all knew he would be. That left me with a quandry. Could I, in all conscience, approach the man? In the end I decided to contact him and play it by ear. It was, after all, the Patient's wish and the money raised was going to the cause which was helping him through his last days. I needn't have worried. The request was granted without question as soon as I telephoned him. When we arrived and were setting up, he came down to see us and we thanked him for his cooperation. " No problem" he said " X contacted me and said you would call and he'd haunt me if I said no"! With just days to live, this man took the trouble to make sure we could help others. People are amazing in times of incredible stress.

Those exercise bike events were great fun. We did shifts of 20 minutes riding whilst the other rattled the bucket. I have to say here that rattling the bucket is frowned upon but hey, I've been frowned upon before. As well as Morrisons, we need to thank Tesco and Sainsburys in Sleaford and Four Seasons Garden Centre in Quarrington. One event sticks in my mind vividly. We were "cycling" in Tesco, Sleaford. The store is surrounded by secondary schools and frankly, we were dreading school chucking out time. Swarms of 14 - 18 year olds with a target to take the razz out of. Oh well. In fact it was an enlightening experience. People who malign the young generation are very wrong. See Chapter 3 rant about Motorists. (That's amazing! I already know I'm going to rant in chapter 3). The youngsters were incredibly supportive and interested in what we were doing. The majority chucked whatever loose change they had left into the bucket which touched us greatly. The effect of those young people touched me so much in fact, that I wrote to the Head Teachers of the schools concerned, hoping perhaps that he could pass on our thanks. Talk about young people not having manners; not one of those Head Teachers bothered to reply or even acknowledge!

Final thanks, I think, go to the fabulous Management and Staff of The Original Factory Shop, also in Sleaford, who went truly beyond the call of duty with staff coming in on their days off to put on an event which raised an awful lot of money.

Please, please don't let me have left anyone out. Our thanks to all who supported us.

Marie Curie reflection.

It isn't easy for some families to give their loved one's care over to a stranger, even one specially trained.

I arrived at the house of patient W, a male in the final stages of life but still aware and communicative. The family was his wife, two sons, one daughter in law and two grandsons. One son showed me into their dining room and asked me to take a seat. He explained that the family were just putting W to bed, he having spent some time in his armchair. I explained that was precisely one of the reasons I was there but he explained that they were used to it and they would call me through afterwards. I was taken through to the sitting room and met Mrs W and the other son. They were clearly tired and equally clearly loved W completely.

They had spent so much time looking after W that they felt only they could manage. I explained again in a very lighthearted way, that I had actually done this sort of thing before and persuaded them to let me take over. Just before they went off to bed, W had a coughing fit which frightened the family and we all dashed through to the bedroom. I rapidly changed W's position to clear his airway and the coughing stopped immediately. The response was memorable. "Ooh, we don't do it that way"! "Does your way work", I asked. "No", followed by hysterical and genuine laughter. The spell had been broken; this bloke knew a thing or two.

Next night I was with W again but instead of the dining room I was shown straight through to W, seated in his chair with the family in attendance. They intended to put him to bed but I persuaded them to trust me to do it, under their supervision because it normally took three of them several minutes. Thirty seconds later W was tucked up in bed without help from anyone other than myself. His comment, also unforgettable, was "you buggers have been pushing and bloody pulling for ages, puffing and panting and creating, then this bloke comes in and does it on his own without any fuss"! "That's family for you W", I replied, "they're just trying to finish you off mate. Well not on my shift"! He laughed heartily and later that evening, when he was asleep and the family and I were in the sitting room, his wife wept openly which was disconcerting until one of the sons piped up, "we've not even seen him smile for months and now you've got him laughing".

Trust is very important when leaving a loved one in another person's care. I became very close to that whole family over the next few weeks and I was present when W passed away. Normally I would wash and prepare the patient myself but Mrs W asked to be there too. We did the job together and at one stage I saw her shoulders shaking and assumed that it was too much for her. When I looked more closely she was actually laughing because in putting on his shirt we had managed to do the buttons up in the wrong holes. "He never could get his bloody buttons right, oh Steve, is it wrong to laugh"? Certainly not is the firm answer to that question and in fact it is surprisingly common. The human spirit is strong and varied and so are the reactions of that spirit to climactic events. Laughter is as good as any.

CHAPTER 3 (Just a short one)

Cyclist v Motorist

You can't have missed the debate going on about who rules the roads. If you've seen half an episode of Top Gear, Motormouth Clarkson will have had his rant.

Having been only a Motorist for the last 45 years I am ashamed to admit that my attitude to Cyclists wasn't perfect. I never did anything dangerous or aggressive towards them but if I came across a large group, riding 3 or 4 abreast, I admit it wound me up. Now I'm a Cyclist too, it *still* winds me up.

Surprise surprise, I remembered something which I should never have forgotten. Cyclists, like Motorists or Christians or Muslims or Chinese or Americans or Black People or Men or Women or People with Disabilities, are members of a group. We are all members of several groups in fact aren't we? I'm a White, Middle Class, Male, Cyclist, Nurse, Rugby Lover, Animal Lover, Grumpy old man etc, etc. Every one of those and every other group, contain people who are good, bad and the vast majority somewhere in between. Please note comments on schoolchildren in Chapter two.

If you're a Motorist who has ever shouted "bloody cyclists", then hang your head in shame. If the Cyclists involved had done something to deserve your anger, you still committed the Cardinal Sin of lumping every single member of a group into the same category. Very, very wrong! If they hadn't done anything to deserve it, you should certainly hang your head in shame, since you are certainly far too aggressive. Take a deep breath and count slowly to ten. Exactly the same goes for Cyclists. I *have* seen Cyclists behave irresponsibly and selfishly. I've been driving towards a bend on a country lane to be faced with Cyclists straddling both sides of the road, pootling along chatting as if they owned the road. _They don't, but neither do Motorists._ We all share the roads. Roads are funded from Council Tax among other things, which we all pay in some form. There is no such thing as Road Tax and hasn't been for yonks, so grow up everybody and treat each other with respect and consideration. These days the roads are dangerous enough with potholes waiting for the unsuspecting. Hitting a pothole in a car is bad enough but on a bike it's potentially deadly. I can't ask motorists enough to please give cyclists room. Even those who it may appear don't deserve it.

Let me touch on cyclists riding two abreast. Firstly it's not illegal. Secondly, it is often the safest way to ride. No wider than a car, shorter and quicker to pass, whereas two cyclists in line could be more than twice the length of a car making it more difficult. All road users need to be more considerate and think more.

Jayne is the least aggressive person I have ever met. There are not enough cheeks available for her to turn; seriously. When she returned from a training ride literally steaming with rage I knew something pretty bad had happened. White Van Man!! The cyclist's deadliest foe. One had overtaken her so close that the wing mirror nearly took her head off! The Hulk appeared from nowhere. Fortunately her clothes didn't shred and neither did she turn green. The overall effect of green skin in ripped dayglo yellow lycra would have been horrible. In every other way though, the Hulk had appeared. Her right foot shot out giving the side of the van a mighty wallop, then the right fist shot out giving it another. She then pursued the offending vehicle for a mile whilst screaming abuse. Fortunately for him, the driver sped off. Also fortunately, the incident occurred several miles from home so any witnesses to her outburst were unlikely to know us.

So what's the rule? Give cyclists plenty of room. Correct, ten out of ten.

Chapter 4. Training gets serious.

We were told that we would be cycling approximately seventy miles per day and would be expected to be able to average thirteen miles per hour. We obviously had to build up gradually to that sort of level and a little beyond, just to be safe. By now it was Autumn and time out on the bike was limited. We joined a local Gym and spent mind numbing hours on much higher tech exercise bikes than ours. We could set gradients for example, although I hated the idea I knew that it was necessary. We went first thing in the morning; me "fresh" from a night shift and Jayne before work. We gradually built up through the twenties, thirties and into the forties. Bloody hell it was boring! Depending on who the duty manager was, we had either the news on television or what I believe is called MTV; very loud music, every track of which had one thing in common. Never the right rhythm for cycling. Either just too slow or just too fast. Happy Mediums are only to be found in seances it seems. After several minutes of being sucked into one rhythm or the other we checked our on board computers and either groaned because we'd been going too slowly and had to race to catch up, or groaned because we'd been going too fast and were potentially heading for burnout.

These gym sessions did achieve the intended result though. We kept going through the winter and continued to build up stamina. It would have been far too easy to drift through and leave everything to the last minute but we were determined not to do that. At our ages, we needed to progress slowly or risk injury which could finish the entire adventure. They also showed us just how fit some people are! One young lady in particular shared our schedule for most of that winter. She was amazing! Early days we just tried not to stare as she ran, cycled and performed miracles of strength and endurance on various pieces of equipment. Over the weeks and months we reached nodding, then brief "hellos" and eventually reached chatting status. This lass would run 3k, it seemed to us almost flat out. Then she'd spend some time doing chin ups and hanging upside down on various ropes and other equipment. This was followed by a vigorous cycle ride at full pelt and then she'd row the Atlantic on a machine. Once we'd reached the familiar stage we asked the obvious question. "Why"? It seems her husband was a Royal Marines PTI and if she didn't measure up when he came home on leave he would drag her out for training of his own design. She decided that the warm gym was the best option!

In early spring we stepped up real road training to forty miles. Despite the gym work we found the roads much

.

harder. One blustery day we set out heading due east down the A52 towards Boston. We had designed another loop which began and ended on the main road but only for a couple of miles in each direction, the rest being on country lanes. It had gone swimmingly and we were delighted with progress. Pride comes before a fall they say. They're right. The lanes we were passing down were all well hedged and we hadn't noticed the wind getting up even further. Congratulating ourselves on a nice run, we turned left back onto the A52 for the last few miles. Into the teeth of a howling hurricane of unprecedented ferocity. It took the breath away, literally and I don't mean a teenagers "literally, I died", or "literally, it blew me away". Actually forget the second one, because it did. Pedalling for all we were worth, we just about managed to maintain forward motion; just! It was Hell. Literally! No really literally. OK of course it wasn't literally but I now see why the word has become so overused. Literally.

The last couple of miles into the teeth of that gale was the closest I ever came to giving up. Seriously, I didn't believe that I could pedal again. I'm not ashamed to say that I actually shed tears. Literally.

I didn't give up obviously or the next words would be "The End". Yes they were the last words then but they aren't now, so shut up!

We live quite close to Rutland Water, which is the biggest man made lake in the Universe. Like the Great Wall, it can be seen from space as attested to by Neil Armstrong when he quoted "One small step for man, one giant lake for mankind". We knew that there was a cycle path all the way around it, so decided to give it a go, making a pleasant change from our usual boring routes. It started well enough until, a third of the way round the twenty or so miles, came a section where the path ran exceedingly close to the water's edge. I dried out quite quickly, it being a glorious day. Other cyclists were constantly overtaking us, particularly on the hilly sections, but I drew the line when two men, one of whom was positively ancient, passed. A couple of miles further on we found them sitting at a picnic bench having a cup of tea. They called out to us as we approached, a witty comment about our pace if I remember correctly, and offered us a brew. We stopped and chatted a while but didn't take the drink. We found out that they were father and son, and that the dad was eighty! I warned the old chap to watch his son closely since it appeared that he was attempting to accelerate his inheritance! It was a very pleasant morning's ride, improved by an excellent lunch at the Noel Arms, Whitwell. The great thing about cycling, or any vigorous exercise I suppose, is that you can stuff your face without guilt. The Noel Arms is the centre of a great practical joke. A few of the locals were chatting about twinned towns for a reason best known to them, when one came up with the idea of twinning Whitwell, population a couple of hundred, with Paris. They wrote to Jacques Chirac I think it was, or whoever was the mayor at the time and without waiting for a response, added "Twinned with Paris" to the road signs at the entrances to the village. They are there still, despite the fact that they received a negative response from Paris, citing the fact that they were already twinned with more prestigious cities.

A while after the Rutland Water trip a colleague of Jayne's, also a cyclist, called with a cry for help. A friend of hers was organising a ride between his local Pub, "The shoulder of Mutton", Ruskington and another "Shoulder of Mutton" in a village just outside Harrogate; Yorkshire. Two riders had pulled out and the event was in danger of being cancelled. "Would we perhaps help out as part of our training"? Of course we would, and there began a day that will live in infamy, the day that we will never forget!

Hindsight is great. Jayne has 20/20, did you know? When we rang "the organiser", he had just got back from Hospital where he had been taken after falling into the river whilst walking to the Doctor's Surgery. Don't worry, he's fine. The river there is only about a foot deep and the greatest danger would be duck attack. The Hospital visit was purely precautionary. He explained the logistics. A team of five riders would be taken to Harrogate in a support vehicle. All five would start from aforementioned Shoulder of Mutton and do ten miles to first stop. Some riders would then jump into the van whilst the others pedalled off for another ten miles. Riders then swapped places and so on until all five cruise triumphantly into the Ruskington Shoulder of Mutton to a rapturous welcome and all the ale you could drink. My sort of welcome exactly. The trip was 125 miles and "the organiser" said that we could ride as much or as little of the total as we liked, Perfect opportunity to get a sixty or maybe even seventy mile stint in?

When I came off the phone, the first reaction was wetting ourselves laughing at the thought of the poor bloke thrashing about in the river, protecting his privates from marauding ducks. Yes, we are bad people. If any of you either are,have been or know nurses, you'll know that we have a very dark (all right, warped) sense of humour. It's essential for the jobs we have to do.

After the laughter we discussed it and agreed that it sounded beautifully organised and would suit us perfectly. The nagging doubt about the suitability of a man capable of falling into a river, on his way to a Doctor's appointment, to organise such an event was pushed to one side. Not a second thought.

As arranged we arrived at his house 04:00 on the big day. We hopped into his car and set off for Harrogate. On the way up he explained that he would be unable to ride today due to a Hospital appointment in Grantham. This caused Jayne a few moments where she had to pretend to be choking to cover the giggles. Perhaps one of the ducks had got through his defences but no, it was a long standing appointment he had forgotten about. Could happen to any of us. Organise a big charity event without checking diary, we've all done it……… He then explained that his intention was to attend the appointment then rejoin us somewhere around the halfway point. Ruskington to Harrogate with us. Back to Grantham to Hospital. Back to Yorkshire/ North Lincolnshire to meet us approximately half way. When I asked about what he intended to do with his car he seemed a trifle vague………..

No matter. We arrived at our departure point and spirits rose immediately because the support vehicle and the rest of the team were there waiting. Perfect planning and coordination. The first stop, ten miles down the road was agreed and the team captain gave a stirring speech. "This is
NOT a race. It's a bloody long way and some of you haven't done any training". I exchanged glances with Jayne. " We'll take it steady and we'll all make it" , he says in his best motivating voice. At this, he shot off like a

greyhound out of the traps, followed by his two mates. Another exchange of glances with Jayne. We knew then that we had been sold a pup. Ten mile relays my arse, we were lumbered with the full distance, 125 miles. We set off gently, intending to discuss it with the others at the first stop. Within a mile of the start there was a beast of a hill. A beast. It used up my entire vocabulary and even then I had to get off and walk. Jayne disappeared into the distance as usual. At the top she was waiting and apologised profusely. Apparently she had been treated with less than due respect of her cycling abilities by one of the guys so she felt it necessary to blast past him on the hill, leaving him labouring in her wake. Respect sister.! At the agreed ten mile point we saw the van, with a little table with drinks and snacks. Excellent! We'd grab a bite, discuss the logistics and get on.

Jayne decided this was a good spot to fall off her bike. She went down with a wallop and once we'd established that she was OK we turned to the bike. *It* wasn't. OK I mean. Several broken spokes and, worse still, mangled gears. She was devastated at the thought of not being able to cycle and we made plans to share my bike. No, obviously not together. One in the van, one on the bike. That way we'd each get a ride. Suddenly one of the other guys said he'd brought his spare bike in the van and Jayne could use that. Fantastic! All's well with the world again. Jayne's bike gets chucked in the van and out comes the spare. To be fair, the guy had said that it wasn't a "brilliant" model. No, not brilliant. Jayne, ever the optimist climbs on. Suddenly the other three jump on their machines, off goes the van and we're alone, Exchange of glances with Jayne; again. No worries, we're mobile. Jayne mounts her trusty steed and finds the saddle in a position suitable for a ten year old. We realised that he had been a little chap and Jayne is not a little lass. No fear. I have my trusty tool kit, Halfords £16.99. Up goes the saddle and we're off. Two yards later I shout Jayne to stop. Rear tyre is flat. Fortunately we find that at least it isn't punctured and inflates perfectly. Obviously, by this time our "team" has disappeared, our waterproofs, food and other essentials with it. I had my mobile phone and, thankfully, my debit card with me.

After another ten miles it became obvious that either the "team" hadn't waited, or we'd gone wrong on the route. This thought was reinforced when we somehow, Jayne's fault probably, ended up going down a motorway slip road! A quick U turn was called for and executed. I phoned the Ruskington pub to find that they had no contact details for any of us. I left my number and explained that we would just make our way back; not to worry. We got a route from good old google and off we went, intrepidly into the unknown. A couple of hours later it began to rain. That horrible drizzly, mizzly cold rain that gets into one's bones. The sort of rain that gets you really wet. You know the sort I mean. We saw a sign for a Garden Centre and, in the hope that a Garden Centre warranting an official brown sign would have a cafe, we turned off. It did have a cafe. Hooray! We went in and ordered a good breakfast and hot drinks. When the waitress had left us, Jayne asked "why does she have a weird accent"? "It's not a weird accent, it's Yorkshire. We're still in Yorkshire". She nearly passed out. "How far had we come"? "How far was left"? Answers, approximately forty and approximately eighty. An expletive which Jayne *never* uses under normal circumstances was barely stifled.

The breakfast did us the world of good. We set off again and even the weather smiled on us; at least it stopped raining. After another couple of hours, somewhere around the halfway point I suppose, Jayne started to feel buttock problems. They are not nice, buttock problems. The bike she was using was, of course, a gent's. She isn't. We are built differently and so are the bike saddles for each gender. Subtle differences perhaps but differences all the same. After sixty miles the differences were becoming less subtle. She pressed on like the trooper she is. We ploughed on through Doncaster, where her gears jammed very nearly chucking her over the handlebars. Trusty toolkit, Halfords £16.99, worked it's magic but Jayne's morale was falling. Bless her, she'd fallen off, she'd put up with a clown's mini bike with a man's saddle and it was getting her down.

Toad in the Hole. It cures anything, well known fact. On the banks of the river, a good old British Pub, with good old British Pub Grub. Toad in the hole with quality lincolnshire sausages, roast potatoes and veg. Aaaah. We were ready to tackle the World and, a great psychological boost, we were back in Lincolnshire and navigating roads we were familiar with.

 It's a sneaky little devil the buttock, or is it two sneaky little devils? I suppose it is in all honesty. You think you've appeased it with toad in the hole but that only goes so far. It lulls you into a false sense of sausage induced security, then bites back. Hard.

By the time we got to Lincoln Jayne was suffering terribly. Twenty five miles to go. Could she make it? I suggested that we take the train from Lincoln, after all we had already done one hundred miles but the stubborn streak is a mile wide. "We'll get some sudocrem and I'll make it". Sudocrem in hand we search for a place to apply it. Don't be clever, I know it's to be applied to the buttocks but where do we find a place for Jayne to extract her buttocks from her lycra without getting arrested. Eventually, Jayne says the equivalent of **** it. At the bottom of a long steep hill leading out of Lincoln are nice big Victorian houses, nestling behind high walls or hedges. Sudocrem in hand she dismounts, and strides through the imposing gates of one such house. There's a rustling of bushes. I'm expecting to hear outraged shouts from inside the house or even, Heaven forbid, from someone working in the front garden. No shouts come, more rustling and Jayne reappears grinning. The remaining twenty odd miles are much more comfortable.

We arrived at the Shoulder of Mutton Ruskington. No rapturous welcome of course because no one knows us. No one knows what we've achieved in their name. Customers were sitting at tables outside and, checking watches, start speculating on the arrival time of their heroes. The fact that two clearly totally knackered cyclists are in their midst doesn't raise their curiosity level one centimetre. I went into the bar and ordered a couple of pints, only to be told that they don't take cards for less than ten pounds. I explained who we were and what we'd done and also that our cash was in the support vehicle." OK, you can pay when they arrive back then", was the generous hostesses response. How kind.

Two members of the "team" didn't finish; one gave up about halfway and the other just three miles from the finish. He must have been in a terrible state to give up so close. We felt for him. The third member came in, accompanied by the van, about an hour after us.

Remember back at the beginning of the day? The "organiser"? Grantham? He obviously got wind of the fact that we had become separated. I'd left my mobile number; remember that? I didn't get a text or a call from anyone. What I learnt afterwards was the oddest thing I can imagine. The dear man obviously had a panic attack and lost his mind. Rather than text me, or phone, he decided to drive back to Yorkshire to find us! Even knowing our start and end points surely makes this a leap of optimism unheard of since Christopher Columbus headed West looking for Asia! Bless him, he was such a lovely chap with massively good intentions and a big heart. Thinking things through was perhaps not his strongest point. He got back to Ruskington about two hours after we'd left for home. In a very generous gesture he made a sizeable donation to our cause.

Looking back it was great. We felt so proud of one hundred and twenty five miles in a day, which set us up perfectly. All we had to do now was do it three days running. Or preferably cycling. Our post on the L2P facebook page was modest in the extreme. Obviously.

Marie Curie reflection.

Any death is sad of course, but being professionally involved generally means that the sadness is contained within. Generally. Here is one occasion when I couldn't hold my emotion in.

I arrived at the Patient's home, which was a beautifully kept permanent caravan on a beautiful site alongside a river. On an archway over the front gate I noticed a wooden plaque in the shape of a Swallow. I know this because it had "Swallow's return" printed on it. The patient was in a very bad way and passed away very soon after my arrival. I hadn't spoken to him once, or done anything for him.

I have mentioned already, that we are there not just for the patient but also family and loved ones. I made a cup of tea and settled down with the new widow. She asked that I didn't wash and dress the body as would normally be the practice. She explained that she had made special arrangements, which of course was fine. We chatted in desultory fashion at first but as she relaxed it became less formal and more wide ranging. I asked about the swallow plaque and she explained that her husband was passionate about them and would sit in the garden each spring awaiting their return and then watch them all summer. When they left for the winter he was always a little sad.

The people with whom she had made arrangements arrived sometime around dawn and they preferred to be left alone. Have I mentioned the time of year? Early spring it was and when I went outside there were hundreds of swallows circling the property. I went back and called the patients widow out into the garden. "Oh, they've come for him", she cried in joy and we both stood there surrounded by Swallows and her husband's spirit. And we wept together. I have no idea why this affected me so deeply but it adds still more to the mystery of who each of us really is.

Chapter 5. To cleat or not to cleat.

That is the question.

My nephew Clive, known as "Boy", was a serious cyclist, thinking nothing of a hundred and fifty miles. Once he found out what we were doing he was full of advice. I refused point blank to shave my legs. I always thought it was stupid; how much wind resistance could hairy legs offer? Stupid me, that's not why they do it. Apparently it is so that when you fall off and cut your legs to ribbons, there is less gunk around to cause infection, easier to clean up and less painful when plasters are ripped off. So there you go. Still not doing it!

One piece of advice he was adamant about was that we needed to cleat up. Cleats are metal thingies attached to the sole of cycling shoes. On mounting the bike, these cleats clip into special pedals, effectively attaching you physically to the bike. The theory is, that one generates power not only on the push down but, being attached, also on the pull up. In my mind however, the obvious downside was that you were attached to the bike. The Boy said that a quick flick of the foot disengages the cleat from the pedal, so no problem.

I decided to give it a try. My first mistake was not realising that there were two types of cleat and therefore two types of matching pedal. Of course I ordered the wrong cleat. Or the wrong pedal, depending on one's point of view. The end result was the same, it wasn't going to work. Once I'd got the correct matching pair it was simple enough to fit. Nifty toolkit, Halfords £16.99.

The time had come. Right leg over and cleat locked in. Left cleat locked in, followed by me crashing to the ground on my left shoulder. The quick flick obviously had to be extremely quick! Not giving up, I got close to our house wall so that I could lean. I practised flicking for a while and felt that I'd begun to get the hang of it. I launched myself forward full of optimism and began to feel pretty good. Frankly, I didn't notice any increase in power but soon forgot about them as I cruised along. I decided on a whim that I'd cycle into Sleaford. Most of you won't know this but Sleaford contains one of the last town centre level crossings in England. In fact they are probably all in Lincolnshire but Sleaford's is special. It closes roughly a fortnight before the train arrives. Once both passengers on the train have dismounted, the gates open and we're off. It was my lucky day though because the gates were open and the traffic lights were green. That's when the Gods stopped shining upon me. The traffic slowed, then stopped. I was alongside a white Transit type van and slowed to a halt.

Did I mention the fact that I'd completely forgotten I was wearing cleats? Alongside the van, I went to put down my foot and it wouldn't move. Luckily I fell to the right, into the side of the van. Desperately trying to release my foot, I caught sight of the reflection in the big wing mirror. From the angle I was leaning at it showed the driver clearly, who was wetting himself laughing. He saw my obviously panic stricken face squashed against the side of his van and his shoulders began to shake. I swear I saw tears in his eyes. I eventually extricated my foot and continued with as much dignity as I could muster. That's correct, none. I spent the next couple of days anticipating a visit, phone call or facebook post from someone who'd witnessed or even, heaven forbid, filmed it. Technology today has left one very little privacy I find.

When I got back home I had a good long think and came up with a great British compromise. I kept one cleat and got rid of the other. This caused massive hilarity once the news got out amongst the L2P gang. I had the last laugh at least three times though. Oh alright, the next laugh twice and the last laugh once since, thanks picky person who pointed it out, there can be only one *last* laugh.

The first of my last laughs came before we'd even left the start line. Waiting for the grand depart in the hotel car park, we heard a crash at the front as the first cleat incident took place. To roars of approval the first rider bit the dust before we'd even pushed a pedal.

Numbers two and three both occurred in Paris itself, in quick succession. In fact one precipitated the other. At a street crossing, a mad Parisian decided to cross in front of the peleton. Squealing brakes followed by screaming people (laughter that is), as one colleague hit the deck, with Karma then kicking in with the ringleader of the laughter brigade joining him on the deck. Sympathy among cyclists for cleat related incidents is similar to the sympathy shown by five a side footballers for ball in testicle incidents. Non existent.

Marie Curie reflection.

I mentioned earlier that there were times when so much love in a home broke my heart. One such occasion stands out. A couple, married as teenagers in the face of much opposition, still very much in love thirty years later and facing being separated by the impending death of one of them. It really doesn't matter which in this case; they were as one. They had a Daughter who worked as a Nurse but who was so devastated by the events that she was unable to manage and considered herself a failure because of it.

I found all this out in the early part of the night by chatting with the Daughter while her parents spent time together in their room. The lass was in such distress that she questioned everything and her anguish poured from her in a torrent. Fortunately, this was an occasion when "letting it out", had a positive effect. Even as she spoke I saw her gain strength and confidence. She would be badly hurt by losing a parent but not broken. Her anxiety about her nursing future melted away as she realised that the doubts were self inflicted and baseless. She was absurdly grateful to me for no reason. I had said hardly a word but perhaps that is what she needed; an opportunity to rationalise without interruption. To square her circles without contradiction. Who knows.

We went upstairs to the master bedroom to see her parents. They were on the bed lying on their sides, she on her left and he on his right. Their foreheads were touching and they had their knees drawn up, also touching. They made the shape of a perfect heart and in that position they both died. One physically; the other emotionally.

I bumped into the daughter several months later and she told me that the surviving Parent was a lost soul, desperate to rejoin the other.

Chapter 6 Team Challenge

Day One

Team Challenge was conceived at a briefing meeting held by the Classic Tours team and the Marie Curie lads. Quite a number of participants came and we met up with some people we'd been in touch with on the facebook page. It was here that I learned that I wasn't the oldest participant, by ten years in fact, but the guys older were all long term, keen cyclists with thousands of miles under their belts; or bottoms, if you will. We met someone we'd been in close contact with on facebook. He had originally signed up to do the ride on a tandem, with his wife. Tragically, she was struck down by cancer and passed away before the event, our friend completed the ride with his Son for support and impressed all of us with his inner strength.

The two stand out attendees were the gorgeous girls Lily and Roxy. They were girls and gorgeous but also absolutely lovely lovely human beings. They were very shy but obviously totally committed. I did what any normal old chap does when he sees two lovely lasses looking a bit lost. I told Jayne that they obviously needed a Father figure to assist them and I'd decided to volunteer. The four of us became quite close on facebook, swapping training and fundraising ideas. They made Big Ben and Eiffel Tower costumes as part of their effort and they looked fantastic! The real bond though, was forged on the first day of the ride and I'll get to that shortly.

The day of departure looming, we began to make enquiries about accommodation for the night before. We were leaving from a hotel in Bexley, so that seemed a good place to start. Don't be stupid, I'm a nurse not an eccentric millionaire! They wanted something over a hundred pounds for the night and about thirty quid to leave the car for four days. Have I mentioned my mean streak? Actually, I'm far from mean. I'll do anything for anyone and give my last tenner to a good cause. What I hate is anyone or any organisation, taking advantage. Thirty quid for taking up a space in what I knew already to be a huge car park, far larger than needed for the hotel, so never going to be full. There were perhaps thirty cyclists staying there, making a nine hundred pound, one hundred percent profit margin for the hotel. No. Not having my thirty quid.

It's important to sleep well at any time. Jayne pointed out that before an early start to a big physical challenge, it's perhaps even more important. I agreed of course but no, I wasn't going to let those thieving buggers get away with it. It's a matter of principal isn't it? I found a bed and breakfast just two miles away which charged thirty quid for the room; yep, the room not just the car park, which was actually free! RESULT!

"It will be fine", I said as we toured the back streets looking for our place, "absolutely fine"! Well it was. Jayne said it wasn't but she's wrong. I believe. It turned out to a row of terraced houses which had all been knocked together. Together is perhaps an exaggeration. Bear in mind that we are on a fairly steep hill here. Although the houses were *joined*, they were not at the same *level*. This led to very interesting, sudden and unexpected changes in floor levels and ceiling heights. I suppose for security reasons, only the two end houses still had functioning doors. Our room, being in the centre, involved quite a trek, several steps and plenty of ducking to avoid low beams, placed where the houses joined. I went to inspect our room, leaving Jayne in the car. "It's fine", I said to the receptionist, whilst my mind was thinking, "I'm dead. She's definitely going to kill me. How can I divert her attention"?

I couldn't. I went to fetch Jayne, my cheeriest "this is fine" face fixed as optimistically as I could manage. She hated it. She hated it so violently that she used that word again. The one she never uses. "It's one night". "It'll be fine". I'm pleading here, can you tell? "If you say It'll be fine once more I'm going to ....". She carried on but I think it best if I leave it at that, we never know who might be reading this do we? I was convinced that I'd be able to get away with it but, sadly, no.   We'd arranged to meet up with various people from L2P for a meal and I began to use redirection tactics on Jayne to get her looking forward to the evening. It was going so well. Bloody receptionist! She chose that moment to knock and advise us that the car park was not secured and we should take our bikes off the car, or risk losing them which would obviously have been very inconvenient. When tackling a bike ride of any sort but particularly long distance, a bike is pretty much the first item to pack. It got worse when we were told that the only place we could leave them would be in our room. Now; have a guess who this is. "I am not carrying that (that word) bike up those (that word) stairs into this (that word) room. If you want them here you can (that word) do it yourself". Advice I've heard several times before, goes something like, if you're in a hole, stop digging. When I tried to point out the obvious advantage that this would save time in the morning her response was …………..how can I put it? Violent sums it up I think. Bitter, that's quite good. Exasperated. Furious. That word!

After I'd carried the bikes up to the room, everything quietened down. We changed quietly. We went down to the car quietly and we drove to meet the others. Quietly. Jayne waited in the car while I went to collect our gang. I tactfully explained that Jayne may not be at her best but she, being the polite lady she is, showed no sign of the previous tension. We had a nice meal, a couple of glasses of wine and everything was fine again; wasn't it? We got back to the room and found that no, it wasn't. It was unbelievably hot. The air conditioning wasn't working because it hadn't been installed yet. The windows didn't open. There was a fan! Woo hoo! It rattled like a runaway train and was also linked to a light of a zillion candle power. Jayne's and therefore my, worst nightmare was coming true. Normally she is a great sleeper. I've known her fall asleep mid word, let alone mid sentence. She's always asleep within minutes. Not this night. I found out that night that she can puff and pant hruff and harumph with the best of us. For the first time ever, I was asleep first but I wasn't going to be allowed to get away with that! An accidental nudge later I was awake. She then promptly fell asleep, *not* followed by me.

I obviously did sleep at some time, because I remember waking up. We went down to breakfast early. Too early because it was shut. We made do with cereal and toast which we were able to sort ourselves. One of us went up to the room to fetch the bikes while the other dumped the rest of the gear in the car. Just as we were leaving, the owner of the B&B came down and saw us dressed in our Marie Curie cycling gear. She immediately refunded our money, explaining that she had recently lost her Mother to Cancer. She and Jayne shared a huge hug on the pavement outside the place and Jayne was heard to say, "wasn't that lovely", as we pedalled off to the hotel to start our journey. I'm almost sure that she meant my choice of accommodation.

On arrival, the hotel's car park was empty as predicted, except for sixty odd yellow clad cyclists. I've left the comma out of that last sentence intentionally, to be inserted in the place of your choice. The excitement mounting we were given a brief briefing. Several L2P coconspiraters asked if they could ride with us, which was nice. Before we knew it, the last year's work was ready to be put to the test. Almost immediately, cleat incident number one, referred to earlier, served to lighten the mood. Our instructions were clear. Follow the high viz arrows. If you haven't seen one for about a mile, you've gone wrong. OK, file that away. We were released in groups of about a dozen, to ensure one huge group didn't block the road for busy commuters. As the groups departed they were sent off with a fanfare of bike bells tinkling and the group responded in the same way.

Purely by chance we were in the final group, but it was not down to chance when that became our position of choice. For choice, read lack of cycling ability. After the first couple of miles the people who had asked if they could cycle with us had disappeared into the distance and never found themselves cycling with us again. The relative positions of each rider became established fairly quickly, probably even before the first of the refreshment stops, which were spaced at roughly twenty kilometre intervals. There is no criticism meant or even implied here, it's Darwinism at it's simplest. There was never any ill feeling between any of the groups which formed, no superiority or inferiority felt or displayed. Before the day's ride, after the day's ride and during breaks we were one group, which just happened to contain several smaller groups of like minded or similar ability riders.

In this way, Team Challenge was born. It was obvious after the first refreshment stop that there were four of us who were, by any standards, the weakest link. Obvious, because we four were arriving after the majority had already left. Steve, Jayne, Lily and Roxy were chatting once their breath had returned and I mentioned that for us four, this was going to be a real challenge, whereas for the rest it was merely a minor and fairly straightforward extension to their usual cycling routines. We were the only ones on basic hybrid type bikes and the only non regular cyclists. I had no idea about bikes any more and was astounded when I found that I could pick up a bike belonging to any of the other participants, using just one finger. With ours I needed considerably more than one. Ten in fact! It was at this point that Lily named us "Team Challenge", a name we carried with pride.

After just half a dozen miles we came to the foothills of the Himalayas, just outside Bexley. The second I saw it I knew that there were not enough profanities in the dictionary to get me up the sheer cliff face which had appeared. Miraculously, cars, buses and other forms of transport were making their way up this beast without tumbling backwards. Impossible! I admit to panicking when I saw Jayne put her head down and attack it! Stupid woman, it's impossible, use your head woman. Gritting my teeth I set off after her, she would need me when gravity got the better of her, sending her tumbling back down to a terrible fate. I managed the first hundred yards or so. It was a vicious little beggar to be sure. I climbed off and started the long slow march of shame. I brightened a little when I saw that Jayne too, had now been forced to walk. If Jayne can't do it, I'm no longer ashamed. At the top we rested. Gradually we moved into the Kent countryside and the day grew hotter and hotter. We were taking the ancient Pilgrims Way and I decided early on that the ancien Pilgrim's could keep it.

When we arrived at the lunch stop we found a lovely pub with a garden by a babbling brook, full of babbling cyclists getting ready to set off again! Hold on, who's eaten all the sandwiches? Emergency rations located, we discovered that it was the first food that Lily and Roxy had eaten all day. Missing breakfast, because they miscalculated the distance to the start point and then arriving at refreshment stop number one too late to get anything but a drink, they were severely undernourished. By now it was in the mid thirties Celcius with no breeze and precious little shade. We pressed on, finding several hills which required us to get off and walk. The four of us were having a self declared break when one of the support vehicles rolled up. To be fair I'm not certain, but I got the impression that we were being encouraged, none too subtly, to grab a lift in the van. Who would know? Only everybody and, most importantly, us! At the end of the ride the Classic Tours guys actually told us that we were the first group in their experience with a 100% finishing record!

I encouraged Lily and Roxy by saying that we were going well but members of Classic Tours said we would be struggling to meet the rendez vous with the ferry. Looking back, I'm sure they meant well but they severely underestimated "Team Challenge". We cracked on into the afternoon and spirits rose when we crested a rise and there, spread out before us was the sea! We were getting close. Spirits were also raised by the fact that several elite cyclists were there at the same time. One, a shapely young lady from Northern Ireland, or Norn Iron as she called it, had fallen and grazed her leg right up to her very shapely bottom. I know this only because she insisted on showing me. She honestly did insist. Really. A very dear friend has been casting a critical eye over my writings and she wasn't keen on the last section. A bit too Benny Hill she said. I've changed nearly everything else she's mentioned, but on this one, all I will say is, Da da da da da dadada da da dadada da dadadadadadada! Incidentally, the ride was well supported by folk from Norn Iron and we also had a Welsh Peleton, including Jonathan, Mari, Tony, Gaz, Andy, Michael and several others to whom I apologise, having forgotten names!

It was here that the gulf in cycling pedigrees became clear. The reason these elite athletes were still there, was that having time to spare, they had taken a thirty mile detour to "pop" to see some place of interest. It didn't matter, we could see the sea, I'd had a glimpse of a shapely Northern Irish bottom and we were going to make it. In truth, we had never doubted that we would make it. We certainly weren't top drawer cyclists by any stretch of the imagination but we'd done our training and we knew we could do it; at our own pace.

The final dozen miles are marred by the nastiest little bugger of a hill right towards the end. We learned later that it wasn't only "Team Challenge" who walked that one! From the top of that hill though, it's downhill all the way. Literally. I don't think I pedalled again until we reached the rendezvous point at Eastern Docks Dover, with more than an hour to spare thank you very much.

We all walked our bikes onto the ferry and I found that the acoustics were perfect for my hooter. Jayne was not impressed of course but many colleagues joined in a final team tinkle on British soil. We locked our bikes and climbed the steps to the much anticipated Restaurant. Before this though, I had a cunning plan. Oh yes. I'd been a frequent flyer on P&O for many years and knew that there were showers on board for the use of truck drivers. I entered the shower area with my "this is my truck driver uniform" face on and as I fully expected, no one gave a second thought. I stayed for a good long while with hot water flooding life back into tired muscles and also taking time to wash my sweaty kit. I changed into casual attire and went to meet my sweaty smelly colleagues for Dinner on the boat. By the time we docked in Calais it was dark and someone had forgotten to clip their lights onto their bike. They had them ready but for some reason the fittings refused to cooperate and insisted on falling off. This resulted in our guide, Gideon (Gideon the guide, that's good isn't it?), getting rather upset with me (Damn, I've given away who it was!). I do feel that claiming I was holding up the Ferry was a bit much.

Once En France, we boarded coaches to take us to our hotel. The overnight stop was in Dieppe, about an hour down the coast, and we were all in high spirits with the first day over with. Once boarded, we were given a briefing about the next day's plans because it would be a late night arrival. "If you have a smartphone don't worry because it will do it automatically but if not, don't forget to put your time on by one hour". I must have been tired because, having been a very frequent visitor to France for many years, I knew exactly what I needed to do but for some reason I listened to the advice. More on this later!

Somewhere around halfway through the journey, Jayne suddenly began to feel very odd. In herself I mean. I didn't stick my hand out and think, "ooh, you feel odd". No, she said to me, "ooh, I feel odd". To start with she was cold, shivering like a…………… help me here someone. What can one shiver like? Anyway, she was shivering. We piled jackets on her to Michelin Man proportions. Then, surprise surprise, she got hot. Very hot indeed. Off came the jackets and several of us were wafting away like Cleopatra's slaves, trying to cool her down. We, of course, ended up on the bus which did not contain the Doctor. We called her and arranged for her to come straight over to us when we arrived at the hotel. We eased Jayne off the coach and found that someone had magically produced a comfy chair on the pavement outside the hotel. She collapsed gratefully into it and slowly began to come around. Her first words confused me, "ooh, a Castle". Was she hallucinating I wondered? Fortunately, she wasn't. There was indeed a Castle, lit up by floodlights, high on the cliffs behind me.

After ten minutes she was recovered enough to be helped to our room. All the Classic tours and Marie Curie staff were very concerned and very helpful. It was suggested that, providing Jayne was fit, we start early so we could have a relaxed ride.

Marie Curie reflection.

I've only ever left a shift once with the following emotion. Shame.
The Patient was a man in his early forties, formerly a keen sportsman and Father to two children aged eight and ten. He was in a very bad way and although I've mentioned previously that we can never be sure, I was expecting him to pass during my shift.

After a restless night where I was constantly changing his position to give greater comfort and trying to ease his distress, he passed away sometime around six that morning. I called his wife and asked what she wanted me to do, then called the required services.

Just before I was due to leave the home, the children came downstairs and their Mother explained that their Dad had passed away in the night.
Understandably very upset the children came towards me and the girl, probably more confident than the boy spoke. "You are supposed to be a Nurse. You were supposed to look after my Daddy. Why did you let my Daddy die"?

Shame isn't the right word of course but I felt very close to it, I felt that I had let them down and it affected me quite profoundly for several weeks.

Chapter 7. Day Two

Once settled in our room, Jayne set about rehydrating and restoring balance to her system. We'd been taking on fluids consistently through the day, as well as keeping well nourished. The heat was almost certainly to blame. It had been well above thirty degrees all day, far hotter than anything we had ever trained in.

With some trepidation I opened the maps for the next day's route. Very helpfully, they contained not only a traditional route map but also an elevation map, showing the ups and downs to come. I nearly fainted! Today had been a really tough ask. We didn't have much left at the end and the route for day two was worse. Much worse. I didn't mention it to Jayne, fearing it could be the final straw in her current state. On the positive side, she was visibly picking up, which helped my state of mind considerably. I set the alarm and we slept like the dead; which is exactly how we felt.

Jayne was up first and clearly recovered. She jumped into the shower while I faffed about. A knock on the door followed almost immediately and our two wonderful Classic Tour girls were there enquiring about Jayne. I feel pretty sure that they were called Lucy and Louise. Please forgive me if I'm wrong but don't forget how old I am.

Stupid too. Whatever their names, they were priceless. My odd sense of humour has come up before I think. Poor Lu and Lu, I'm sure that's what we called them. Without opening the door, I replied to their enquiry about Jayne's health with, "I'm really sorry to have to tell you that Jayne sadly didn't make it through the night. She went very peacefully though and of course I'm used to preparing bodies so she's all laid out nicely".

A sharp intake of breath from the other side of the door was followed instantly, from the bathroom, by; "he's a git! Ignore him, I'm fine thanks"! A miracle, obviously. The girls roundly abused me for several minutes once I'd opened the door. Such fun! Now then, who remembers the time changing incident from earlier? We were very pleased that we were good and early to grab breakfast and get underway with a head start. Oh no. Stupid me suddenly realised what I hadn't realised the night before. Not every smartphone changes automatically and I knew all along that mine didn't! Not my fault I explained to Jayne, it was that Classic Tours bloke, he told me wrong. Of course that didn't wash. Nor did I as it happened because we had to get a move on. Excellent buffet breakfast thrown down we went steed hunting. All the bikes were laid out on a green in front of the hotel. For one horrible moment I thought that an old fashioned Le Mans start was planned. For the uninitiated, the drivers all lined up on the opposite side of the road to their vehicles.

At the sounding of the starting gun, they galloped across the road, jumped into their cars and whizzed off. Quite a spectacle it was too. The problem was that there was no handicapping system employed. Clearly some drivers could run, as well as drive, faster than others. After several disastrous years where the slow runners got mown down by the sprinters in their midst as they got their cars started and thrashed it out into the road, the system was changed to a less exciting but safer one.

Sixty odd people milling about in search of their machines was quite fun to watch. We had no difficulty at all; ours were the stone age beasts which stuck out a mile. We eventually got going and set off towards Jayne's castle. Great news though! Chatting to the Classic Tour guides I mentioned the fact that today looked at least as tough, if not worse than yesterday. They were amazed when I mentioned it, saying that it was a nice fairly steady day. When I showed them the map there was initial confusion, until someone spotted that the scale was different, making it look much worse than it was. Hooray.

It turned out to be a very nice days ride. Still very very hot, well into the thirties but through beautiful rolling countryside much of it following a small river valley. The nicely maintained French byways rolled by under our wheels like a smooth conveyor belt and we felt good. Bucolic. The first time I saw that word I wasn't sure. It sounded a bit like a condition or illness, "He's gone down with his bucolic again poor lad". At that time of course I actually had no idea what it meant and admit to being surprised when I looked it up. "Idealised country life", it said or "relating to shepherds and herdsmen". Since then I've adopted the word and use it regularly. Bucolic, there it is again.

First stop was in a lovely small town where we snacked in the shade of what was originally a market place, by it's appearance. Several of the professional types had a major detour planned to visit a local Chateau, would we care to join them? How much distance does the detour add seemed the logical question. About fifty kilometres being the answer, the logical response was; NO THANKS! Team challenge continued to potter along at the back but remaining well within any time constraints. It was here that I had my encounter with "The Doctor"! She was a very nice lady of course and we felt gratitude to her for caring for Jayne the previous evening but I was about to be totally baffled by her. "You are another stupid one", she said to me without preamble. I was lost for words. Yes, I know, but it's true I swear it. "Stupid"?, was my quick witted response. "Yes stupid", she repeated. She pointed at my bicycle lock which was wrapped around the stem of my saddle. "There's no need for you to be carrying that extra weight, you should take it off and leave it in the support van". I started my response several times, searching for the right words and just as importantly, the right tone. In the end I thought, **** it. "I weigh a tad short of seventeen stones. My bike is the weight of a small family car and you think the weight of a bicycle lock is going to make any difference"? There was another word in between a, and bicycle and also between any, and difference but leaving it out is best for all concerned and doesn't change the sense at all. I fear the tone was the wrong one. In hindsight, it could have been construed as aggressive, although that wasn't my intention. Exasperation is what I was looking to convey. Never mind. She never spoke to or came near us for the rest of the trip, although I'm sure that was coincidental. Sorry Doc.

 It was also at this stop that we continued and cemented the friendship with our "Pirate" friend Jonathan. In order to prevent sweat running down his face and soaking the inside of his helmet he wore a bandana tied around his head, giving him the piratical look once his helmet was removed. Aaaarrrggggghhh, was the obvious comment, so it was made. It was returned with interest and became our regular greeting through the ride and ever since.

Onward through the glorious countryside under wall to wall blue skies. There was a section of swooping downhills followed by very short climbs leading to another swoop down long winding hills. For perhaps five or six kilometres I pedalled no more than a dozen times. It was invigorating and gave us a massive sense of freedom. This was beginning to feel comfortable. Easy even? Lunch was in, or perhaps at, is better, a typical French village bar set opposite a picturesque old church. I changed in to at, because there was room for no more than a dozen people inside and because the weather was so gorgeous, it was better outside anyway. The buffet was generously laid out on tables outside and was set upon with gusto. I love using that word, mainly because my Stepson is named Gus and called "Gusto" by me. Every time I am able get the word in, I can imagine Gus setting upon a buffet or getting stuck into a rousing song or wherever I've managed to squeeze it in. I know I'm sad, no need to say it. And now I realise I lied. About the Doc. I have a very cunning way of eating hard boiled eggs. Cold ones of course. You make a smallish hole in the narrow end and a larger hole in the fat end. You then blow hard through the small hole and the egg pops out through the big one. Who wouldn't be impressed by such a feat? The Doc was flabbergasted and gathered a group to watch me repeat the performance. I was filled with pride when it was agreed by all present that it was the most amazing thing they had ever seen. I am available for Weddings, Birthdays (except kids. I hate kids) and Bah humbugs. Is that what that Jewish thing is called, Bah Humbug?

The various groups began to drift off after a lovely hour lying in the shade of the Church and catching up on who had fallen off where and when and why. Cleat incidents being the most common, followed by gravel skids. Team Challenge, being mounted on sensible heavy bikes with nice wide tyres, never had gravel skid problems. That and the small distance we covered on rough ground or cobbles, was where we shone. Not long into the afternoon we reached a hilly section which we negotiated without walking, much to my personal delight. One section, through an immaculately kept village full of very expensive looking homes, had the smoothest Tarmac I have ever seen. This hill was adorned with speed bumps every ten metres, the strange thing being that the bumps were on both sides of the road. The downhill section we could understand, but why the uphill? It seemed pointless. This was a question that Lily asked as she struggled up the hill and over each of the offending lumps.

"Why"? We heard from behind. "Why"? Then, ten metres later, "why"? Another ten metres, "why would you put speed bumps going up a hill this steep"? Ten metres later, "are they stupid, why"? Ten metres later, "there's no need, why"? Ten metres later, "whose idea was this"? Every ten metres up that hill. Jayne and I found it hilarious and inspiring. It was Lily's much politer version of me swearing at hills and abusing them. She reached the top without dismounting so it clearly worked for her. That was the worst incline of the day and before we knew it we'd reached the hotel for night two.

Once we'd showered we lay down to take stock. Hell, we were two thirds into it, well almost. Tomorrow was a longer ride but according to our Bible, contained only one serious climb. We could do it. We really could. Dinner that night was a high spirited affair, the feeling that we were confident of completing the task was clearly felt by all. We sat with two people, Jonathan and Mari, who became good friends. Jonathan and I had as previously mentioned swapped banter and insults over the two days and we certainly had similar sense of humour, much to Mari's disgust. I happily led Jonathan astray and we had such a great time that I couldn't even begin to guess what we ate. Not a clue. We shared a couple of bottles of red, the four of us, almost equally. I feel sure and the whole group had a roaring night. Back in our room, Jayne suggested a plan so cunning, with an outcome so outrageous that I felt sure she had been put up to it. She wouldn't do this herself surely? Big build up followed by big let down. We decided to get up early and get off before the elite riders knew what had hit them. Aaarrrgghhh.

Marie Curie reflection.

Another example of how amazing the spirit of people can be in times of trouble.

I arrived at the patient's home to be greeted by the lady of the house. Her first action was to apologise for wasting my time but her husband had passed away a few minutes earlier. Apologising for her husband's death putting me out!

I went inside and I did the final checks and prepared him for the Funeral Directors. It became clear that neither she, nor her family who had arrived in the meantime, were at all aware of the procedures. We sat down with a cup of tea and I went through the drill, from Funeral Directors, registering the Death, and the myriad of other red tape. Their faces were blank throughout, plainly too shocked or emotional to take it in. When I asked if they had chosen a Funeral Director and received a negative they obviously needed even more help. We discussed the local services available and they decided to go with the Co-operative Funeral Service, which was well thought of in the area. They asked me to make the call and to wait until they arrived, which was fine.

Whilst waiting, the rest of the Family turned up, including Grandchildren. After a while a Grandson aged around eight, sat on Gran's knee and snuggled up tight. How sweet. He then said, "Granny, you aren't going to get married again are you"? We all laughed of course and when Granny assured him that she had no immediate plans, he was so relieved. "But why"? asked Gran. "Because Aunty Andrea is getting married and she keeps saying how expensive it is and if you had to spend your money on a wedding, you'd have less to spend on Christmas Presents"!

Not much floors an eight year old!

This story also has an interesting post script. I left the home between three and four A.M. Just after leaving I realised that I had not followed procedure by phoning the Marie Curie control centre to tell them I was mobile. The organisation takes the security of their nurses very seriously and we all have trackers with emergency buttons. The downside of this, is if one forgets and the tracker is somewhere it shouldn't be, or isn't updated. I recall once being woken up by the sound of the front door being battered by the Police, because I'd forgotten to update and I'd gone into Emergency Mode! So, I needed to update and, being a good citizen, pulled up to make the call. As I did so I noticed a Police car go across a junction ahead of me but thought nothing of it. Call completed I set off again but within a couple of minutes blue flashing lights behind me, belonging to said Police car, urged me to stop. A young WPC approached the car so I obligingly slid down the window. I'm a Law abiding chap, man and boy, and object to being addressed as a criminal or suspect. I'm also a naughty awkward cuss at times!

"Do you have a good explanation for driving around at this time of the morning Sir"? She asked. My response seemed reasonable to me, "do I need one"?
"You were behaving suspiciously Sir and you car isn't registered locally".
"I'm sorry for behaving suspiciously, could you explain exactly how it was suspicious please"?
"When you saw the Police vehicle, you pulled up to let it pass and then continued, why were you avoiding contact with the Police"?
"I pulled up before I saw the Police vehicle, not because of it, and I continued because I had finished the thing I had stopped for".
"Why are you being difficult Sir"? "Because I'm a man", but with this I produced my Marie Curie I.D. and she put down her taser. That last bit isn't true…the rest, sadly, is

Chapter 8. Day three.

Up with the lark, we breakfasted alone. Careful not to disturb anyone we retrieved our bikes and were gone, like a thief in the night, Mwahaha. It was another glorious morning and we felt great. After half an hour or so, Jayne voiced the big question. Now, we all know that the big question should never be voiced. The second it's voiced, it's ruined. "Do you think we could get to the first stop without being overtaken"? At this point of course we were leading day three of what she had suddenly decided was a race! What glory awaited us? I was about to answer when Chris Graham, a man of few manners and no principles, flew past us. Badly brought up quite clearly. Jayne voiced her displeasure at Chris's departing backside and he turned to say, "don't worry, there's a whole gang coming up fast"! Swine.

It was at about this point that Jayne decided she needed to, you know, spend a penny; tinkle, you know. We soon found a suitable spot in a small clump of trees. I don't believe I've mentioned so far that we were wearing what is known in the cycling fraternity, as bib shorts. Essentially it's like a woman's one piece bathing costume. This, of course, makes the aforementioned penny spending quite awkward, having to remove the whole garment before having the freedom to perform. Fortunately I'd chosen the perfect spot and she achieved the desired outcome without problems. We leapt back onto our trusty steeds, determined to give as good a show as possible at the first checkpoint. There was a moment of panic as we arrived, Jayne forgot that we were on the Continent and swerved across into oncoming traffic! She received a blast from the horn and angry yells through the open car windows . Fortunately Jayne speaks no French but it wasn't nice; at a lady too! We managed to arrive safely in tenth place according to Jayne's calculations and after the initial disappointment of not winning she accepted it like a man. Or woman, in her case. She accepted it, like a Lady. She also then realised that she'd left her sunglasses at her ablution spot! No! We were not going back for them.

At this point I leap forward two years. We have taken a short break in France and nostalgically retraced part of our route using a sensible mode of transport. The car. Suddenly I recognise the terrain, it all comes flooding back. That very stand of trees is up ahead of us, I recognise it for exactly the same reason I chose it two years previously, it's a perfect spot to tinkle. Jayne is convinced (again) that I've lost my mind as I screech to a halt. Well I stop anyway. I point out where we are and she too recognises the spot. She was out of the car in a flash and galloped to the trees every bit as quickly as she had when she really needed them. She got to the spot and there, on the ground at the side of the tree, was a coke bottle. You didn't seriously think did you? Honestly? Jayne was actually disappointed not to recover her glasses! Two years Jayne. Perfect tinkling spot. As Sam Goldwyn once famously misquoted," we've all passed a lot of water since then", and I'd bet my life that a lot of it was behind those trees.

Miraculously, we're back in 2014 as if nothing had happened. Karma is wonderful isn't it? The instant kind even better. Chris Graham, badly brought up bloke, remember, decided to make a solo breakaway attempt. He checked with the van driver at the first stop which direction we were heading and took off in search of victory. The van driver had forgotten which way he was facing and pointed Chris off in the wrong direction. Remember earlier on that we were told, "if there are no signs after a mile, you've gone wrong"? Remember? Chris who, being badly brought up, hadn't listened, and ploughed on for miles. The van driver suddenly remembered that he'd sent some poor schmuck off in the wrong direction, so set off in pursuit. If you listen to their two versions of the tale, you'll find they have everything in common but the distance covered. Each time Chris tells this story he's done another five miles before the van catches him, thinking it gains him sympathy. Wrong Chris, what the rest of us think is that it's such a shame his Mum didn't teach him to listen to simple instructions and to think, "hang on, I haven't seen any direction arrows for a while. Never mind, crack on"! To his immense credit Chris refused the offer of a lift back to the starting point, not wanting to appear to have cheated and not wanting to ruin the chance of a good story.

The ride between the first stop and Lunch was through more of the lovely Normandy countryside to a rather plush Golf Club. That told me immediately that we were nearing Paris. Golf isn't huge in France, with courses scattered only around the big cities. Lunch on that third day was intended to be a bit of a treat I suppose, a sit down meal in nice surroundings. It actually turned into a bit of a farce. Whether the place wasn't up to it, or whether the organisers hadn't done the maths properly I don't know but the meals arrived piecemeal, pardon the pun, with some people still waiting for starters while others had finished main course. They also ran out of the intended main dish, Jayne and I being the unlucky last recipients of a truly terrible lasagne. Those still waiting were treated to a beautifully prepared steak with frites and salad. Apparently it was delicious. I bet Chris Graham got one. Swine.

The afternoon ride took us gently into the suburbs of Paris, with excitement mounting as we approached our goal. We reached a long fast descent we had been warned about previously. At the bottom was a sharp bend, which apparently catches out many careless riders who frequently end up in the front garden of the house on the apex. We all got round unscathed and we crossed the Seine for the first time. For a reason I don't understand, the Seine can't decide which direction it wants to head in. It makes frequent changes of mind and continually turns back on itself. We were heading in a reasonably straight line, yet still crossed the river several times. This isn't a complaint of course, crossing the river was wonderful and allowed teasing glimpses of the City. We had a final rendez vous in the Bois de Boulogne before trundling towards the Eiffel Tower.

The group had become very strung out due to a proliferation of roundabouts and traffic lights splitting the groups. Somehow we managed to be amongst the first arrivals in the Bois de Boulogne. It became obvious very quickly that we were not the only people using the spot as a meeting point. At this point I am legally required to issue a Parental warning. The following section contains sexual content and flashing images.

Ladies of the Night, I learnt that day, also work during the daytime. There were three or four very shapely young ladies wearing um,,,,,,,,,,, very little. What they did have on was short, extremely tight and accompanied by very high heels. Have you got the picture? It was apparent that we were trespassing on business premises and we were slightly concerned that we would be asked to move on, as having potential put off customers. Not at all. This is France after all and they have very different attitudes to "that sort of thing". It wasn't long before a car pulled up, negotiations took place and driver and businesswoman headed into the woods. I've no idea who started it but someone started tinkling a bell. Not big or clever or funny. More bells followed, rising to a cacophony which could only be enhanced by a good old hoot from me as the happy couple disappeared.

After almost an hour we were one group again and set off on the final couple of miles. The Eiffel Tower popped out from behind buildings now and then to start with but, as we got closer it stayed hidden behind the surroundings. This was where cleat incidents referred to earlier happened. I recall now that they were also related to the sight of a beautiful E Type Jag which helped distract the victims. One of our number, a lovely Japanese chap who came on the ride with his wife, later had a picture painted of the scene and sent it out to the L2P team. It is a great shame that my computer crashed shortly after our return and I've lost their details but they were charming in the extreme. I'm not keen on racial stereotyping, particularly of course when used negatively, but they really were impeccably polite and actually did give little bows when saying hello. Adorable and obviously committed because they were not European based but had made the trip from Japan specifically for the ride.

As we got nearer the tower we came across another UK based Charity group cycling in the opposite direction. "Not far now", one of them shouted across helpfully. "You don't know where we're going", I yelled back without thought. For some reason a couple of our riders reacted as if this was the funniest thing they had ever heard, nearly falling off their bikes laughing. I love an appreciative audience as much as the next man but felt that it was more down to hysteria or heatstroke, than the quality of the repartee!

As we stopped at the traffic lights in the shadow of the Eiffel Tower, a female voice behind me said, "we've only gone and bloody well done it"! It just *may* have been Holly. I'm not certain but the fact that I heard it so clearly above all the Parisian traffic makes me think it perhaps was. I'm not saying her voice is loud……..

The atmosphere was euphoric, obviously. Several riders had family members there to greet them and there were many emotional scenes. Hugs, handshakes and congratulatory kisses all round, followed by zillions of photo ops of elated cyclists holding their bikes above their heads. As previously mentioned, my bike lock weighed more than their bikes. I mentioned to Jonathan that the only reason I would resort to lifting my bike above my head was to chuck it in the river! His response, quick as a flash was, "don't do that Steve, it would be In Seine". I wish I'd said that. Considerably better than, "you don't know where we're going"!

Marie Curie reflection.

Midge. Midge. Midge. There's only one and if you've met her you remember her. She was a Marie Curie nurse who contracted breast cancer herself, fought it off and returned to Marie Curie and St Barnabas Hospice.

The only thing bigger than Midge's heart is her mouth. No, even that isn't as big. I adore every bone in her body with every bone in mine, and so does Jayne. Rough Diamond was a term perhaps invented for Midge. She is the only person I have ever met who swears more, in normal conversation, than I do. We both know it's not big, clever or anything else but we like it. Shock value perhaps, no idea really. We are with Billy Connolly in his assessment of people who claim we swearers lack vocabulary. "**** that", he says, "I know loads of ********* words but I like these ones best"!

Imagine my concern then, when I find I'm following Midge into the home of Roman Catholic Priest. The Priest lived with his Sister, who was the Patient, and her two daughters both of whom were nurses. That isn't always a comfortable situation, having other nurses around. They, understandably, hover around with eyes digging into the back of one's neck, ensuring you're doing the job properly. As I said, understandable but off putting. So to recap, Roman Catholic Priest, two nurses in the family, one dying Patient and one inveterate swearer Marie Curie nurse; what could possibly go wrong?

Nothing. That's the answer. The Priest was enough to make me wish I'd kept my religion. Down to earth, amusing and witty, yet compassionate and caring. The two nurses were from the same mould; adorable. I joined the family in Prayer while the patient went to sleep and the priest asked if I was Catholic. "Not a very good one", I replied and his response was lovely, "we none of us are Steve, none of us". I sat with the family and Midge was the topic of conversation, as I'd feared. But not in the way I'd feared. They *adored* Midge like I do, giggling like school children when telling me of their conversations. They covered everything it seems, including religion, and the priest smiled fondly as he recalled some of Midge's retorts. You see, it isn't only what you say that matters, it's the way you say it.

If I could grant anything in the world to anyone, it would be whatever Midge wanted.

Chapter 9. The Celebration Dinner.

Once we'd had official group photos and people had exhausted their imaginations of their own photo taking opportunities, including a special one of Team Challenge we all, some more reluctantly than others, remounted our bikes for the last couple of miles to the hotel.

After a shower and change of clothes, we had a couple of hours to kill before the big dinner. Jayne and I elected for a wander around the City, something she will never get enough of. Just after we met, in 2007 Jayne told me she didn't like France, having had a miserable time there when she was a teenager at a swimming event. Oh dear, that's a problem because I have always been a francophile and actually harboured a desire to retire there, which of course you already know actually happened. Ruining the story won't stop me finishing it. I somewhat nervously booked a weeks holiday but obviously it all turned out well. On our first day I took Jayne up to the Basilica of Sacre Coeur. Paris is situated in a natural bowl with hills surrounding it, and Sacre Coeur is on one of these hills. We climbed the steep steps to the front of the beautiful building and I asked Jayne to turn around. She gasped as she saw Paris laid out before her, basking in glorious sunshine. The Eiffel Tower, Napoleon's Tomb and many other famous landmarks were there and she had no idea where to look first. She was in love at first sight. We spent that day walking mile upon mile and that was it; hooked.

So on that extra special day we had another walk around, very slowly, located the Restaurant for the evening's extravaganza and returned to the hotel to change.

The Restaurant's ambiance had us hooked immediately. I'm no expert but Art Deco would be my guess. Gorgeous place with mezzanine floors on two levels, We had the whole of the first floor to play with and Jayne and I, experienced travellers that we are, chose a corner table not too far from the toilets. We were joined at the table by two fellow riders, one of whom was Chris Graham, the badly brought up one. Truthfully, he was immaculately turned out in his DJ and, providing you promise not to tell him, he's actually a fabulous chap with a great sense of humour and quick wit. He has become a friend for life and has already been across to visit us in France a couple of times. The table was completed by John, another splendid chap with an equally great sense of humour.

I can't recall what we ate, which is testament to what a great night we had. The meal was excellent, I do remember that much, and was washed down with copious amounts of good red wine which ensured a great atmosphere. The atmosphere was so good that the customers from the third floor came down to ask us to quieten down. They realised immediately that they were on a loser. The wise words "you don't spit into the wind" didn't need to be voiced, it was plain for all to see. In a splendid example of bending before the inevitable, they dropped their complaint and came down to join us!

After coffee and liqueurs came speeches. There were several awards decided by the Marie Curie guys which were presented. They included an award for the person who fell off most, which I believe was won by the lovely Susan who, incidentally has the nicest, politest and cutest daughter imaginable. Ian I believe won the best dressed rider and, I'm delighted to say, there were awards for all four members of Team Challenge! Lily and Roxy received an award, for downright determination I think, and Jayne and I received an award for, "The couple most likely to have their own TV series". Quite what that means we aren't sure, but we've taken it as a positive thing, having no evidence to the contrary. Before Dinner, Pete and Dan had asked me if I would say a few words, being the first time they had ever had a Marie Curie Nurse actually take part in the ride.

I'll now do my best to recreate the speech as accurately as possible.

" I'm sure that many of you were horrified to hear that I am a Marie Curie Nurse. This big brash bugger though, is only the cover of the book which, as we all know, should never be judged. Open up the book and there is a big softy inside who cares more about people than you can imagine.

As the first Marie Curie Nurse to complete the London to Paris challenge, Peter and Dan have asked me to speak to you about what a Marie Curie Nurse does. This will touch a few raw nerves I know but it's the reason we are all here. I'm sorry if I open wounds barely yet closed but I want also to share some hope that your loved one's last days and hours were made better because we were there for them.

There's no such thing as a good death but there are such things as horrible deaths, We are there to help prevent those horrible deaths, so people don't die in pain, soiled or dirty, unkempt, in need, in discomfort and worst of all, alone. We are also there for the families and loved one's of patients, for whom this is often their first experience of loss and who also need both emotional and practical support.

I'll share a night shift with you. I arrived to find the patient surrounded by family. Well meaning family as they mostly, but not always are. It was clear to me but not them, that the patient was distressed by all the commotion going on around her. Using my best, let the Nurse do his job voice, I cleared the room and sat down with the patient and reassured her that peace would reign from now on. She relaxed immediately and I left her for a few moments to explain gently to the family that, in their understandable and commendable desire to help, they were in fact doing the opposite. Having heard it, they immediately realised the truth and were mortified, so I had to reassure them that no harm had been done but what was required was peace and calm. They agreed to go to bed because they too needed rest. Then they asked the understandable yet impossible question. Will she live through the night? I explained that I never attempted to make that guess, because that was all it could possibly be. I've attended Patient's who seemed so close to the end that it seemed unlikely they would last the hour, yet carried on for several days. I've also seen the opposite. Then followed the second understandable but impossible question. You will be sure to wake us if she's about to go? Again impossible, sometimes we get a sign, often we don't. Sometimes we get what we feel may be a sign which isn't. I'll do my best but can make no promises.

Back with my Patient I sat next to her bed and took her hand, she shouldn't be playing cards in her condition! (Too much continuous sad chat risks losing the audience, so chuck in a laugh. The brackets are me talking now, not part of the speech and the audience appreciated it!)

So I took her hand and she gave me a weak little smile. "You won't leave me will you"?, she asked. "I certainly won't", I reassured her and she drifted off to sleep. I sat holding her hand until, in the early hours she woke and gave me a glorious smile which lit up her face. "You didn't leave me did you"? "I promised you didn't I"? She dropped off again and slipped peacefully away, without warning, a few hours later. I woke the family, who came down. The first comment was from her Daughter who said, " she was at peace, you can tell that". Mission accomplished".

So that was me finished and looking around I saw, as I feared, tear stained faces everywhere. Most of the owners of those faces then came over to give me a big hug, it was a very special emotional moment.

After the speeches and presentations were finished, the four of us from our table spent several hours strolling around Paris where coincidentally we kept tumbling into bars containing other London to Paris colleagues. I have no idea when but someone suggested a burger. Stupid idea. When you've had a skinful it has to be either curry or kebab, it's the law. Curry in Paris is available but not widely. Kebabs on the other hand are ubiquitous thanks to the former Colonies and Territories in North Africa. We found a kebaberie very quickly. Have I mentioned that we'd had a few drinks? We were extremely happy. We'd achieved something very special, we'd had a great meal with copious wine, we'd had a tour of Paris bars and we were boisterous. Not nasty, not aggressive but perhaps a little noisy. The staff in the kebaberie were really nice but kept asking us to be quiet. Quiet? It's God knows what time in the morning in a still open kebab shop and they expect quiet? It turned out that their family lived above the shop and were sleeping, so OK we were quiet. We sat outside munching, chatting and making suggestions for the next challenge which the four of us would take on together. Gradually, the L2P gang drifted back and eventually we staggered to bed.

Certificate of Achievement

This is to certify that

Stephen Marsh

completed the London to Paris Cycle Challenge

24 - 27 July 2014

in support of Marie Curie Cancer Care.

Fabian French, Director of Fundraising

Marie Curie
Cancer Care

www.mariecurie.org.uk

Certificate of Achievement

This is to certify that

Jayne Marsh

completed the London to Paris Cycle Challenge

24 – 27 July 2014

in support of Marie Curie Cancer Care.

Fabian French, Director of Fundraising

Marie Curie
Cancer Care

Marie Curie Cancer Care

Certificate

This is to certify that

...... *STEVE AND JAYNE MARSH* ......

Won the

MOST LIKELY TO HOST THEIR

...... *OWN TV SHOW* ......

On the

London to Paris
Cycle Challenge
24th - 27th July 2014

Chapter 9. Back down to Earth.

We rose surprisingly early that Sunday morning and felt fine! We'd booked an extra day in Paris, so said farewell to a lot of our colleagues and most poignantly, to the other half of Team Challenge. After breakfast we headed off to Montmartre and once more climbed the steps to Sacre Coeur. Since that first visit, Sacre Coeur has always been Jayne's favourite place and we visit every time we're in Paris.
Adore it as we do, there is one thing which marrs it and it's the same at all the main tourist sites. Thieves, beggars and con artists. Keep everything secure and either ignore or give a firm "bugger off", to anyone who approaches you with anything. Don't take anything off anyone, don't hold your finger out and let a man tie string around it to show you a trick, don't believe the girls who come up with signs claiming they are deaf/ dumb, don't fall for any of the dozens of tricks they get up to. Also beware on the metro, or more precisely on the escalators. A favourite trick is for a pickpocket to jump on the escalator and a colleague then hits the emergency stop button. In the confusion Mr Pickpocket picks pockets.

Anyway, this Sacre Coeur moment was extra special because Jayne had asked all her friends and colleagues to write down the names of anyone they had either lost through Cancer, or who was fighting the battle. We joined in the early Mass, which brought tears to Jayne's eyes. The beauty of the Nun's singing and the Priest's chanting was both haunting and inspiring. Religious or not, I defy anyone not to be moved. It's a spine tingling, hair on the back of the neck raising, butterflies in the tummy moment. When in Paris it's a must do; trust me. You don't have to stay for a Mass, there are concerts there and often groups of Nuns, (is there a collective noun for Nuns I wonder. A convent-ion perhaps?), rehearsing or maybe just singing for the joy of it. The acoustics are so incredible it is magical. At the end of the service we went to a side chapel and lit candles in the names of all the people on Jayne's list and left it for the Priests to mention in their prayers. We left feeling wonderful and ready for lunch.Another must for us, when in Paris, is lunch Chez Gladine. It's a restaurant specialising in Basque and Catalan regional dishes rather than the more traditional French cuisine. It's a fantastic experience providing you like mucking in and aren't up yourself. You would not choose it for a romantic assignation, or to take granny for her birthday, or go with young children, all of which are just some of the reasons we love it so much. It's a collection of non matching tables, chairs, stools and benches thrown together in no discernable order. The menu is written on a blackboard, the serving staff mostly students and you often end up sharing a table with total strangers. If you do try it, you won't stay strangers for long. There's nothing like fighting over the last piece of bread in the basket to bring people together. I did really have an "argument" with a lady when she picked up the last piece of bread. "No, no that's my piece", I said to her. Her initial reaction was surprise, then puzzlement and her face began to change until her husband, realising I was only playing, began to laugh. We had a great lunch together and came away with an invitation to stay if we were ever in Paris again. Ever in Paris again, of course we will be, Jayne can't go more than a year without seeing it. By the way, you'll never run out of bread Chez Gladine, it's on tap as it were.

Some words of warning.

1.If you aren't there by 12:30, you aren't eating lunch. It's full by then and you need to yell your name to the Patron and tell him how many of you there are. He'll shout back to acknowledge he's got you on his list and then you hang around until space clears and he shouts you. I guess you're beginning to see why I say not to go there if you're a bit up yourself.

2. Don't be fooled by the word "salad". The salads Chez Gladine come in huge stainless steel dog bowls and will comfortably feed a family of four.

3. Don't be fooled by the appearance of the staff. No uniforms (I don't mean naked, just not waiter/ waitress traditional Paris black), no pads and pens or other waiter like accessories, but stunningly efficient, ever friendly, always ready to help if you're unsure of anything and I'm fairly certain that they are all descended from octopi since they can carry so many different shapes and sizes of dishes without ever coming close to losing control.

Chez Gladine is Restaurant, meeting place, cabaret and a window into Paris. We love it!

Second only to Sacre Coeur for Jayne is the Eiffel Tower. She has an actual physical need to go up the tower every time she's there. Sometimes the queues are unbearable, so here's a tip. You can book a tour which shows you around the underground tunnels and bunkers around the tower where you see the engineering and the history of it's use as a broadcasting station in the early days. It's a fascinating trip in itself but the bonus is that you then get priority entrance, without queueing, and access to areas of the tower that ordinarily you wouldn't get. We do it every time now because it costs very little more than the standard entrance and I hate queues. I abhor queues. I say to Jayne that I can't think of anything worth queueing more than half an hour for; I'd rather not do it. We once paid to go to a theme park, can't remember which one, and everywhere we went were signs saying " queue from here is one hour", **** that. We went home. To be fair, Jayne would have stayed and queued but not me. Never.

After the tower we hit the river. The Seine is a major thoroughfare through Paris, with river buses and taxis ploughing up and down around the tourist boats. We took a boat from the Eiffel Tower to Notre Dame and, most excitingly, took our very first selfie! Get us! We were surrounded by Japanese tourists selfieing for all they were worth and we saw, for the first time, the now ubiquitous selfie stick.

We walked back from Notre Dame past the bridge whose name I've forgotten, where lovers fit padlocks containing their initials to the railings. It began many years ago on just one bridge, which is now full, so lovers are spreading out to other bridges. It is now becoming a bit of a nuisance and recently a whole section of railings fell into the river.

Throughout the afternoon the streets of Paris began to fill. The Tour de France was coming to town, finishing on the Champs Elysees that evening. We couldn't decide whether or not to attend but in the end our stomachs got the better of us and we decided to eat; again. We like eating, so there. I had a beautifully tender juicy steak and Jayne had her all time favourite, Coquilles St Jacques.

Jayne loves a Brandy. I don't. The waiter's face when I refused the Brandy we'd ordered and pointed to Jayne was a picture. The Woman drinking Brandy and the Man not! Sacre bleu, I wager he's still in shock.

So the last night of our adventure came to an end. Back to Blighty and back to work.

Chapter 10. Welcome Home

Those of us who had booked the extra day caught the Eurostar on the Monday morning. We disembarked at Ebbsfleet and took a taxi back to Bexley to be reunited with "Boris" and "Oh Shit". Some shuffling was now needed. Our kit had, understandably, been deposited with the bikes at the hotel, whereas our car was at the superb bed and breakfast I'd tracked down. This gave Jayne another opportunity to revisit the controversial choice and Jayne is never one to resist a second chance. I got it again; both barrels.

We were doubtless suffering from something for which there is a name but, as I don't know the name, I won't use it. It involves the feeling one gets when you've achieved something special and aren't quite sure what comes next. Whatever it was, it manifested itself in grumpiness. It began with the overnight choice and I soon provided further ammunition by not fixing the bikes onto the carrier properly. There was a noise we didn't recognise coming from the back of the car, bumping and scraping. Boris was dangling and bouncing along behind, giving Jayne second wind. This provided enough ammunition for the Cold War to last as far as Peterborough. The ice began to melt as we got closer to home and finally thawed completely when we pulled into the drive. Friends had bedecked the front of the house and garden with ribbons in blue and yellow, the colours of Marie Curie, and welcome home banners.

The entire village turned out to welcome us home, or it could be that our arrival, coinciding as it did with the arrival of the school bus, came at a time when more than the usual number of people were on the streets.

What now? Suddenly our time was our own. No training. No fundraising. How on Earth would we fill our days? What we did was return to work and wonder how in hell we had made the time to do anything else!

The ride was an inspiring event and we were determined to continue cycling. My determination lasted a week. One single ten miler and that was me, finished. Jayne, Teacher's pet, continued regularly and actually asked for a "proper" bike for Christmas. She's the owner of a lovely white Claude Butler racer, liftable with one finger.

We heard from Lily and Roxy soon after our return, with pictures of really beautiful matching tattoos celebrating the achievement. I'm not a massive tattoo fan but these were really gorgeous pieces of art. They inspired me and I had one done myself to record the event. Just a small outline of a bike with the dates and "Team Challenge". The facebook page continued and we kept in touch with many of our friends. The idea began to circulate of a reunion ride. Fantastic idea said a couple of dozen people, we're in! When? That whittled it down! Where? That whittled it down a bit more. Eventually, we hosted the ride in July 2015, at our home in Lincolnshire.

Steve, Jayne, Ian, Lily, Chris, Mari, Jonathan, Pete Lee, Jill (Noddy), Peter and Pippa all gathered chez Marsh on the anniversary of the final day. Sadly, I was too busy to participate in the actual ride, being in charge of putting out the direction arrows and setting up a refreshment stop and all manner of administrative duties. Shame. The chosen route included sections of our training rides and took in the village of Surfleet, famous for it's leaning Church. Severe subsidence has caused one end to sink dramatically. Who needs a leaning tower when you can have a complete leaning Church. As it happens, the church is opposite a very nice riverbank pub and, equally coincidentally, we were passing by at lunchtime. Rude not to don't you think? I spoke to the lovely landlady to arrange a selection of snacks and sandwiches and, yet again, I was astounded by the appeal of the Marie Curie cause. The landlady gave a generous donation as well as a discounted buffet. The Mermaid Inn, Gosberton Road, Surfleet, take a bow.

The programme for the evening was a barbecue. I'm very proud of my oil drum barbie. Big enough to cook a pig if needed, with grill plates attached to chain pulleys, allowing up and down movement for regulation of temperature. We had the usual barbie stuff; Lincolnshire Sausages, (the best sausage known to man, as you are aware), burgers, chicken, prawns, whole pineapple and a leg of lamb. Once the lamb was cooked, we found that amongst our number was an expert carver with huge experience. Thanks to Peter, all we were left with was a clean bone. What a talent.

What's that? Pineapple? Of course, the best ever barbie pudding. Several guests, including badly brought up Chris Graham, were amazed at pineapple on the barbie. Peasants! It's fabulous. Chuck it on whole, keep it turning to ensure even cooking and then slice it. Simple and delicious, the cooking brings out the sweetness and gets the juices flowing. Everyone stuffed to the gills, it was time to turn the barbie into a bonfire. I brought through an entire pallet, intent on chucking on as it was; whole. The assembly was in uproar; you'd think I'd never done it before. It was worked out exactly, the pallet being a perfect fit for my oil drum beauty, and I lowered it on gently and produced a roaring fire, throwing light and heat around the garden.

Being the exact matching weekend, we were then able to watch the finish of the Tour de France, with Chris Froome clinching his second win.

The weekend had been a great success and our guests left with high hopes and talk of further reunions.

As yet no other reunions have materialised of the cycling kind. As previously mentioned, badly brought up Chris has visited a couple of times in France and was actually responsible for me getting back on "Boris". The three of us had a couple of jaunts while he was here, which led to a funny email exchange and even funnier finale from Chris. I mentioned that, because of jayne's new bike, we had three available so we could try a little pedal if we felt like it. This led to the following exchange of messages, not necessarily word for word.

Chris. Excellent but won't be able to pack a helmet but I'll risk it without.
Me. Wear it! There's always a nutter on a bus trip and if you wear it they won't come and sit next to you!
Chris. Well that's not going to happen because that would make *me* the nutter.
Me. Wrap the helmet in tinfoil then, if anyone asks you can tell them it's to protect your brain from microwaves and suchlike coming from space. That way the reason for the helmet becomes sensible.
Chris. No.

On his arrival at the bus station there he was, cycle helmet on, covered in tinfoil, looking every inch the eccentric. I think that's what I called him.

Jonathan and Mari visited, sans velo, in Lincolnshire as did Pippa, Peter and Pippa's husband whose name now escapes me completely because we only met that once and because I'm old and incontinent. Sorry, incompetent.

Chapter Eleven

Final thoughts.

Some of you will know that I had a diagnosis of Cancer a few years ago and had successful surgery. Jayne too had successful surgery and chemotherapy, so we have been two of the lucky ones. We certainly feel very grateful for our outcomes but it confirms our desire to help the cause of those fighting cancer.

I hope the Marie Curie reflections acted in a positive way, that was my intention. After years in money grabbing business, my working life finished in Social Care and Nursing, which I care about passionately. It is a field which is in a mess and getting worse. I fear for the future, but Jayne says I can't rant, so I won't. The work I did with Marie Curie was the most rewarding I could ever imagine. People said to me, "it must be terrible, knowing that everyone you see is going to die". Firstly, we're all going to die; just not yet. I understand the question on one level but on another, I have to say "that's precisely why we are there". Human Beings, certainly Western Human Beings, are not programmed to talk about or even consider, death. It's Taboo but shouldn't be. It is one of the two certainties in life after all. The fact that we are there as much for the families and loved ones of the patient is also paramount. When they receive the news, where do they go? Who do they talk to? How should they react? Because of our Taboo, no one wants to talk about it. No one dares to mention it. People cross the street, not because they don't care, but because they have no idea what to say. But people in that terrible position need to talk. To try to make sense of things. To learn how to react. In my reflection of patient W, I mentioned laughter. Mrs W felt guilty for laughing but need not have. That home was filled with laughter; always. Why not now?

"Is that wrong"? One of the most common questions a Marie Curie nurse is asked when families react. Other than the situation described in my one negative reflection, the answer is always, NO! There is no "right way" to react when you lose a loved one, neither is there a "wrong". It may surprise many of you when I say that laughter is actually very common. One night I attended a family where the daughter was due to be married within a couple of days but sadly her father died that evening. I asked the family if they wanted me to prepare the father for the funeral director, to wash and dress him. They replied that they would and when I asked if he was to be dressed in a smart suit intended for the wedding, the response was No, "put him in his Arsenal kit". I washed the gentleman and realised very quickly that this kit had been purchased when he was considerably younger and slimmer! It was a fight I promise you. An epic battle, but I got it on him. I was pouring in sweat, uniform soaked in it when I came out of the room. There, swigging tea on the settee, was the family and *two* Marie Curie Nurses; all wetting themselves laughing! Apparently, my efforts at disguising my "quart into a pint pot" struggles had failed, to the amusement of the family. When my "colleagues" had arrived, the family pointed to the room and told them what I was doing. They listened for a while, "he sounds like he's got it covered, we'll have a cup of tea and wait"! The sight of me, dishevelled and dripping in sweat, emerging from the room was too much for them to contain!

I was invited to many funerals, which was nice, but difficult. Working night shifts meant that I had very little free time, with training, fundraising and sleep all craving my attention. I attended two. Those I couldn't miss. One was George, my

Arnhem veteran and the other was H, a lovely, lovely woman with an equally lovely husband. Midge and I both attended the funeral. I mentioned that Midge had been hit again with cancer and was going through chemotherapy at the same time as Jayne. They both lost their hair and reacted differently. Jayne said "nuts to you" and went around bald as a coot. Midge had a cold head so opted for a wig. At the funeral Midge's wig, rather like it's owner, refused to behave. Every time she stood to sing a Hymn, it drooped to the left, covering her eye and giving her a very saucy "come and get me" look. This had no effect on me as you will imagine. Not at all. Tears streaming down my face and shoulders shaking, I attempted to maintain decorum while Midge tried to wiggle the wig back into place. What could possibly go wrong? She succeeded in shaking it down over the other eye too, turning her into a singing Old English Sheepdog. Have I mentioned how much I love Midge?

I'd love to come up with some wonderful deep and inspirational thoughts at this point. Really deep and inspirational. Ummmm.
It appears that I can't. Sorry. But I know a man who can...........

"Forget all the reasons it won't work and believe the one reason that it will." – **Unknown**

"Challenges are what make life interesting and overcoming them is what makes life meaningful." – **Joshua J. Marine**

"It's hard to wait around for something you know might never happen; but it's harder to give up when you know its everything you want." – **Unknown**

"One of the most important keys to Success is having the discipline to do what you know you should do, even when you don't feel like doing it." – **Unknown**

"Good things come to those who wait... greater things come to those who get off their ass and do anything to make it happen." – **Unknown**

"Chris Graham has been badly brought up and will only end up teaching French and supporting a terrible Rugby Team"! – Steve Marsh

Jayne wants me to say that there were many times when she questioned her ability to complete the task we'd set ourselves. I'm not going to say that though. I truly believe that she was always capable of it and, in her deepest, maybe unconscious mind she knew it too. I may have mentioned before, that she is the most stubborn being on the planet. Nothing short of serious injury would have stopped her, or ever will, from doing something she'd set her mind to. We are all capable of great things, not that cycling from London to Paris is a *great* thing of course, but the year of graft which went into getting us ready *was!* The five people quoted above, all knew what was required. I find it interesting that four are unknown, maybe because so many different people claimed to have said it that it was called a draw. I can say without fear of contradiction that I have at last come up with one of my own. "Never, in the field of human cycling, has one man spent so long staring at his wife's ass disappearing into the distance, and not contemplated giving up".

The wave of exhilaration which swept over us beneath the Eiffel Tower continued, Tsunami like, for a long time after. Many months later and even now, four years on, it continues. The memories of the pain and anguish are long gone, (easy for her to say, not mine. Mine will never go) leaving behind only the soft warm glow of contented success. We often refer to those times, always retaining a sense of awe at what we, two old codgers, had managed. Whoever you are, or however misguided you must be to be reading this drivel, you are capable of something and we urge you to get off that ass and do it. Anything. Just do it.

Finally of course, I want to mention all Marie Curie Nurses. The work they do is incredible. They are simply the best. Better than all the rest. Bar none.

17806741R00066

Printed in Great Britain
by Amazon